BUUR - LATZ - SSSS - GREISCH
zone noord

ORG - ARUP - CG - DELTARES
zone noordoost

BANISTEN
ING - COBE
ne west

SIN4E - NDVR - H-N-S
zone oost

AGENCE TER - TVK - ARCADIS
zone zuid

STUDIO PAOLA VIGANÒ
CRAFTON ARCHITECTS - MAARCH
zone zuidoost

Overkappin
Ring Oost

MOVEMENT

AMBITION
CHANTER
WISHLIST
NEEDS
OF
COMM

INSTITUTIONAL CRACKS

EXPEDITION
RING.

AWARENESS

UNIVERSITY

RESEARCH

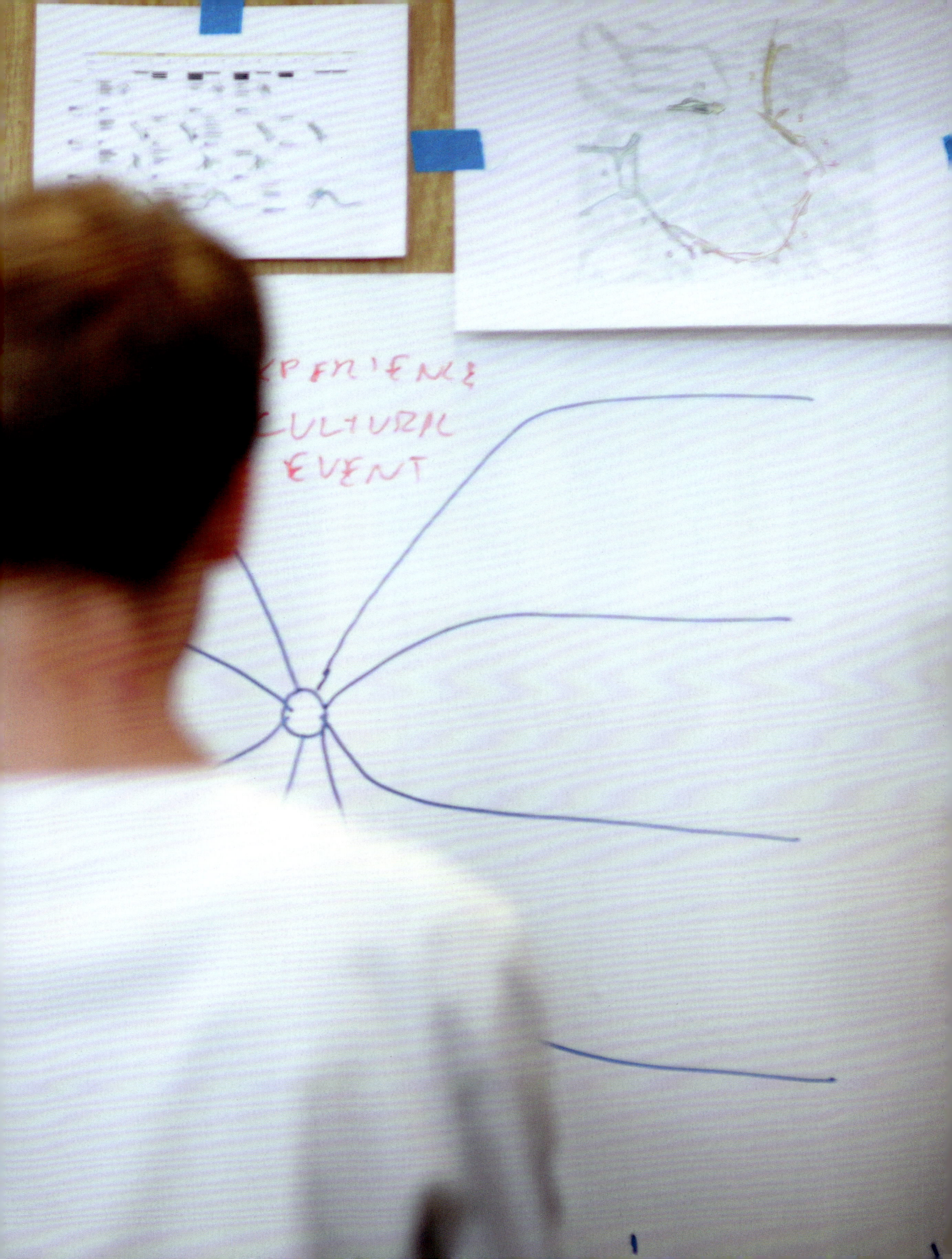

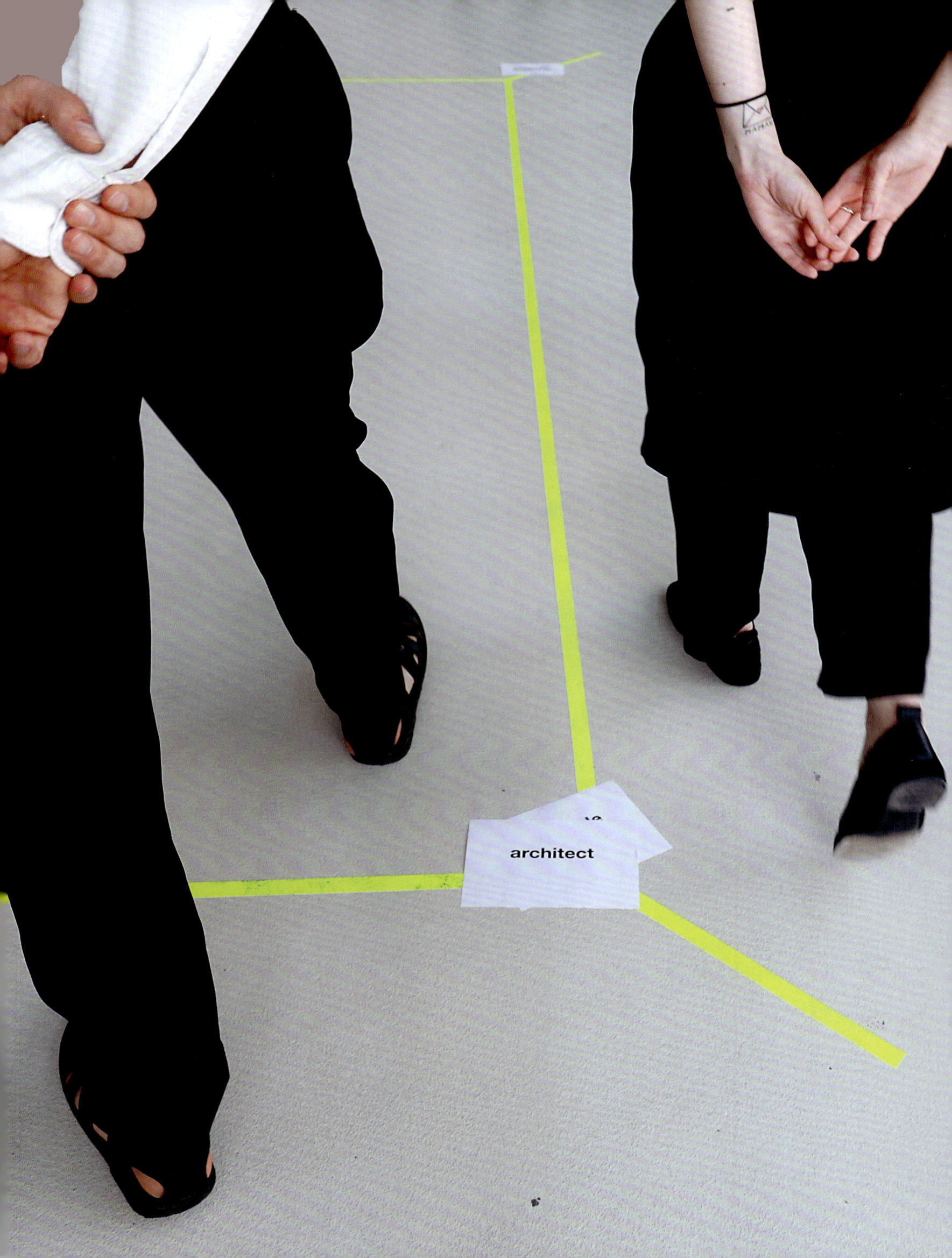

After working together on several projects, it became clear that, although being three different kinds of offices, 51N4E, Denkstatt and Endeavour share a similar attitude. Curious about this common way of thinking we decided to launch a research trajectory at the chair of Architecture and Urban Transformation (ETH Zurich) and to trace underlying dimensions of what we have come to call 'design in dialogue': an expanding notion of architecture that pays tribute to reality by valuing complexity and diversity of opinions.

Based on different interviews, workshops and re-enactments of our past experiences we tried to make our expertise tangible and open for discussion. In this first part, six dimensions of design in dialogue, that were developed along the way, are presented and illustrated by projects by each of the three offices.

These dimensions, one could also say ingredients, must be understood in the context of a stable and fairly comfortable status quo, already occupied by multiple and often parallel realities. Reflecting on our work is an attempt to question and to clarify the room for manoeuvre that architectural practice has.

Part
I.

Design in dialogue

Dimensions

1. Out of necessity
2. Knowledge of the many
3. Safe ground for learning
4. Risky experiments
5. Senior improvisor
6. A culture of cooperation

"One of our first projects was to design a swimming pool that looks like a pond in the garden of the courtyard farm of my parents. It might sound somewhat silly, but this project has been a hinge point. And it has been so for several reasons. We had to reconcile the ideas of my mother and my father. That proved to be challenging. My father almost drowned once and does not swim; my mother loves water.

Instead of locating the pool in the garden, we proposed to build it in the courtyard of the farm, in the heart of the building, bordering my mother's dance studio and my father's office. Having the pool there transformed the entire building. It introduced a fragile sense of intimacy; an awkward kind of vulnerability that invited visitors to open up."

FREEK PERSYN, 51N4E

"Design in dialogue arose as a method to focus on the relation between things, rather than on things themselves. In times where complex issues tend to cause isolation and defensiveness, we hope to do the opposite: connecting the stakes of administrations, citizens, experts and users through the design of urban and architectural projects."

JOHAN ANRYS, 51N4E

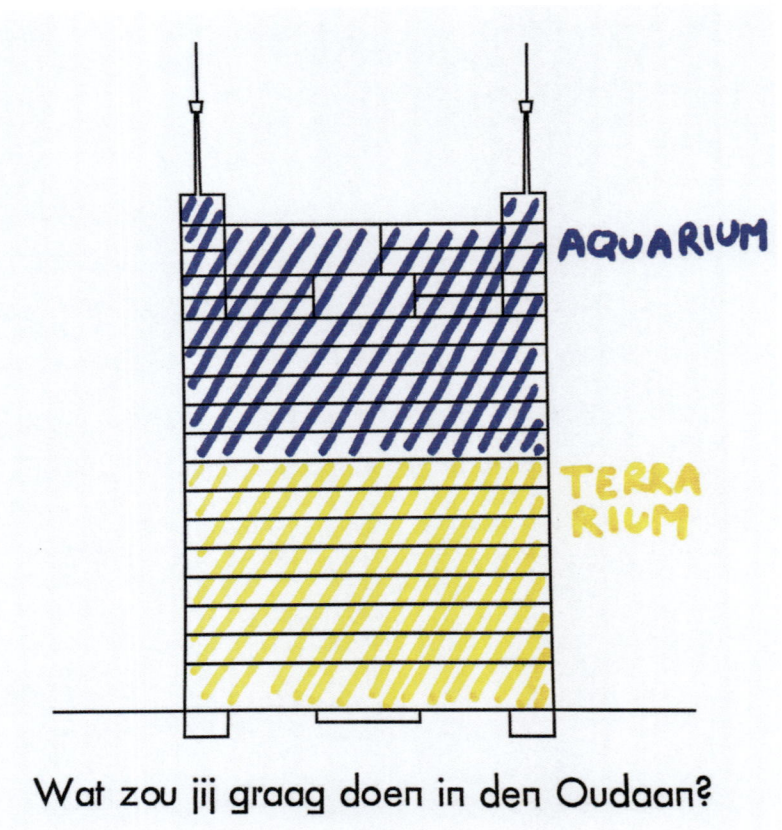

AQUARIUM

TERRA RIUM

Wat zou jij graag doen in den Oudaan?

"A couple of years ago we tried to buy an office building that housed the police force of the city of Antwerp. *Den Oudaan*—as the building is known by the locals—was designed by the modernist Belgian architect Renaat Braem in the 1950s. With its fifteen floors it is an iconic, brutalist landmark in the heart of the city."

MAARTEN DESMET, ENDEAVOUR

Burgerinitiatief ijvert via Facebook om de zeventien verdiepingen tellende Oudaan te kopen

't Stad is van iedereen, en de politietoren ook

Een groep jonge Antwerpenaren wil de iconische politietoren in het centrum van de stad kopen en renoveren. Concreet zijn de plannen nog niet, de interesse des te meer. 'De Oudaan moet weer zijn plek krijgen.'

ANDRIES FLUIT

€ 10,5 miljoen

▶ Zoveel bedraagt de vraagprijs voor de Oudaan

E en paar vrienden ontdekken vorige week dat het zeventien verdiepingen tellende toren te koop staat. Ze beslissen om hem niet zomaar uit handen te geven aan een projectontwikkelaar en richten vrijdag een Facebook-pagina op. 'We kopen samen den Oudaan'. In een paar dagen tijd verzamelen ze 2.500 geïnteresseerden. "Dit leeft bij zowel de culturele en creatieve sector, als bij een aantal mensen uit de vastgoedwereld", zegt stadsplanner Seppe De Blust, een van de initiatiefnemers. "Allemaal vinden we dat het gebouw van de stad moet blijven."

De Blust en zijn kompanen, een zevental Antwerpenaren van rond de dertig, willen dat het gebouw vooral meer wordt dan zomaar een gebouw. "De klassieke manier van ontwikkelen, zoals op het Eilandje, kan op architecturaal vlak nog wel meevallen, maar heeft meestal geen grote meerwaarde voor wie niet in die buurt woont. Met de Oudaan willen we de maatschappelijke impact weer opkrikken."

> 'We willen dat de Antwerpenaar de schoonheid van het gebouw weer ziet'

SEPPE DE BLUST
INITIATIEFNEMER FACEBOOK-GROEP

Wat die impact is hangt af van de noden van stad en omgeving. Die kunnen betaalbare huisvesting zijn, een ruimte voor cultuur, een plaats voor jonge ondernemers, maar ook nood aan verbetering van de ruimte rond het gebouw zelf. "Nu is het nog een politiegebouw met een betaalparking ernaast. Een erg afgesloten publieke ruimte dus, terwijl het een schakel kan zijn in het centrum van de stad", legt De Blust uit.

De betonnen Oudaan staat bij de Antwerpenaar niet meteen te boek als een architecturale parel. De Blust denkt daar anders over: "We willen dat de Antwerpenaar de schoonheid van het gebouw weer ziet. We kunnen er een nieuw centrum van maken, met een mooie groene ruimte errond. De Oudaan moet weer zijn plek in de stad krijgen."

Voor de invulling rekent de groep op ideeën van onder meer burgers en handelaars uit de buurt. Daar heeft De Blust als stadsplanner al ervaring mee. Hij adviseert met zijn collega's van architectenbureau Ndvr overheden en hoe ze bij stadsplanning lokale actoren kunnen betrekken. "Door aan crowdbuilding te doen kun je zulke projecten verbeteren. Je kunt concrete afspraken maken, bijvoorbeeld rond autogebruik en parkeernoden en zo de ruimte efficiënter benutten."

Coöperatieve

Het uiteindelijke plan is om een coöperatieve op te starten die voor de concrete uitwerking moet zorgen. En voor het geld. De vraagprijs voor het gebouw aan de Oudaan is 10,5 miljoen euro. Een hoop geld dat de initiatiefnemers bij een aantal grote spelers en particulieren willen halen. "Er zijn grote partners geïnteresseerd, waaronder een vastgoedbedrijf en platformen rond creatief ondernemen", zegt De Blust. "Aan de reacties op Facebook merken we ook dat veel mensen bereid zijn om mee in het verhaal te stappen."

De huidige bewoners, de Antwerpse politie, verhuizen in 2018 naar een nieuw gebouw. Dat moet deels gefinancierd worden met de verkoop van de toren. 25 maart 2016 is de uiterste datum om op het gebouw te bieden, dus dat geeft de groep nog negen maanden de tijd om het stadsbestuur te overtuigen. De stad is niet op de hoogte van het initiatief, schepen van Ruimtelijke Ordening Rob Van de Velde (N-VA) laat wel weten dat alle partijen die een rechtsgeldig bod doen, een kans maken.

Welke vorm de participatie precies moet krijgen, willen De Blust en co. de komende weken uitwerken. Dan moet duidelijk zijn wie welke inspraak krijgt, al dan niet afhankelijk van de investering. Maar ook hoe ze zullen beslissen over de indeling van de toren. Op de Facebookpagina gaan de voorstellen alle richtingen uit: van appartementen en betaalbare kunstateliers over een boerderij op het dak tot een café en een klimmuur. "Het zal een uitdaging zijn om tot een compromis te komen", geeft De Blust toe, "maar we hebben nog wel even tijd."

▶ De initiatiefnemers van de Facebook-groep 'We kopen samen den Oudaan', met stadsplanner Seppe De Blust in het rode T-shirt. Achter hen: de bewuste politietoren. © ERIC DE MILDT

DM
Cult
▶ 8
De burger roept, en zal niet meer zwijgen

"In the end, we didn't buy the building. We didn't even try. A last-minute change in the bidding procedure sidelined us. But the whole experience made us aware of the thrilling sensation of an idea gaining momentum in the public sphere once it captures the imagination of the general audience. It made us realize we could run an office and be activists at the same time—and we've been dancing on that tightrope ever since."

TIM DEVOS, ENDEAVOUR

Basler Zeitung

Freitag, 8. Oktober 1999
Nr. 235

Teil II   Die

Das Aus für Sulzer-Burckhardt in Basel

Die Kompressorenfabrik Sulzer-Burckhardt, die bisher in den Werken Basel und Winterthur produziert, gibt den B.
Beschäftigte verlieren ihre Stelle. 140 Personen, davon 80 Grenzgänger, sollen neu in Oberwinterthur arbeiten.

Ende 2000 werden im Sulzer-Burckhardt-Werk im Gundeli keine Kompressoren mehr gebaut.   *FotoPD*

Basel/Winterthur. Ein weiteres Basler Industrieunternehmen schliesst: Im Rahmen des vom neuen Sulzer-Konzernchef Fred Kindle angekündigten Stellenabbaus legt Sulzer-Burckhardt (MSB) seine zwei Standorte in Basel

soll versucht werden, die dringend benötigten Spezialisten an Bord zu behalten. So erhalten Informatik-Spezialisten die Möglichkeit, teilweise zu Hause zu arbeiten. Den MSB-Beschäftigten soll ein Teil der Pendelzeit als Arbeits-

ren Arbeitgeber in Basel oder bei MSB in Winterthur. Die zwei Bereiche «Standard Hochdruckkompressoren» und «Vakuumtechnik», in der ohne Administration 70 Personen beschäftigt sind, sollen möglicherweise verkauft

war für da
gemischter
Gewerbe)
Teil des G
Denkmals
Burckhard
den. Sie w
Jahren, in
griert.

Als
schlechtest
SMUV-Sel
Entscheid,
nicht einsi
mensberat
bis heute i
her imme
dass der F
che. Das
letzten Jah
auch imme
die Börse
massiv Ste
Münger.

Qualifizie

Mit d
terthur ver
zialplan zu
Er glaube
seien, nach
gehen. Ge
ger sei das
der Alu M
trams in ei
rere regio
schliessen,
Region für
mer nach
Die MSB

"As with many good things in life, luck played its part in the development of Gundeldinger Feld. It started with an announcement in a local newspaper and a chance encounter in a supermarket."

BARBARA BUSER, DENKSTATT

"Today, twenty years later, Gundeldinger Feld feels like a living room for the entire area. Somehow, people managed to claim this space and make it their own. We are privileged to see the joy it brings on a daily basis. It fuels our desire to continue bringing people and ideas together and firmly rooting them in places that radiate a spellbinding energy."

ERIC HONEGGER, DENKSTATT

Design in dialogue

23

1

Out of necessity

Firmly rooted in a long, diverse and interdisciplinary tradition of education varying across institutes of arts, humanities, engineering and life sciences, the field of architecture has always been characterized by a sense of curiosity and an eagerness to influence cultural and societal patterns.

Architectural practice is filled to the brim with attempts to challenge, empower, restrict, or question all kinds of social behavior. Its discourse is conversed with fierce debates and tumultuous political discussions. Some of the contemporary concerns are, for example, the rejection of suburban living, the societal and environmental impact of building materials or the cultural value of heritage sites. Projects become attempts to materialize bits and pieces of these grand narratives, well aware of the fact that their actual societal impact is unsure and beyond control.

One of the reasons for the strong difference between the architectural dream and what is actually realized, is the fundamental social nature of the profession. In essence, architecture is a collective process. Architectural practice relies on others, both for the realization of projects and their actual use, and for the shared hope of the building outliving its creator.

This view consequently implies active exchange with others and involves more stakeholders in increasingly complicated processes of decision-making. A closer look at everyday architectural practice shows however that little space is given to take this role of a mediating collective practice seriously. An overwhelming number of procedures, demanding technicalities, and the ever-present competition between offices, leave no room for architects or other urban practitioners to question the added value of the whole operation or to further specify its greater ambition.

It is precisely this field of tension—the threat of unquestioned selectivity inherent to architectural practice—that characterizes the necessity of design in dialogue. In a society still struggling to overcome the fragmentation caused by modernist management models, design in dialogue strives to break new ground. Instead of accumulating introverted technical expertise whose implementation in projects often fails the practical test of the unpredictable reality, it advocates for more room for manoeuvre—and it does so, not for the sake of the profession, but because the result of their efforts will be more resilient when people work together.

Zentrale Pratteln

Directly north of the Pratteln train station (Switzerland) on the former site of the Coop distribution center, the non-profit housing association Logis Suisse AG will develop a lively district with residential and commercial uses. Also, the municipality of Pratteln plans to build a new school complex on the site. Denkstatt was asked to define a framework, communication strategy and identity of this district under transformation. Through a strategy of persistent permanence (cultivating the model of the concierge) the project became a laboratory for the integration of logics of transitional use, hybrid programs and a careful exploration of existing qualities of the building. In response to a classical logic of development, Denkstatt created the room for manoeuvre to introduce a culture of experimentation and to preserve parts of the building from demolition.

01   Oven baked pumpkin served at a dinner of the local Denkstatt team. Permanence became a key tool to make things work and quickly connect a variety of ideas and actors.

A critical attitude

In a project like Zentrale Pratteln, design in dialogue will not guarantee a more inclusive or democratic form of urban transformation but it creates the conditions to actively question what is happening. Moments of dialogue give everyone involved the possibility to assess the ambitions and logics of a project and to continuously raise questions. Who is involved? Who decides? With whom can I collaborate? How do I organize myself to support this collaboration? What is the specific role of design in this process?

This reflective nature of design in dialogue makes it to what can best be described as a critical attitude. It is an approach that allows to make the design process a shared concern and to create the right context to question underlying mechanisms of urban transformation. In the case of Zentrale Pratteln, the careful process of collectively tracing the history and potential uses of the site and the organization of different experiments to challenge or resituate already defined programs, allowed to rethink, in conversation, how living and working can possibly merge.

02   A challenging condition for the transformation of Zentrale Pratteln is its size: 4,5 ha and 60,000m² of floor area. Such a large surface is not easily developed and creates opportunities for Denkstatt to enter the game and experiment with possible alternative transformation strategies.

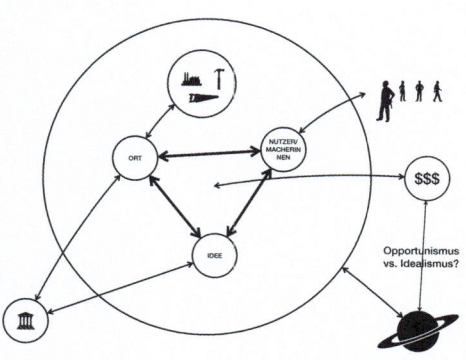

03   A place, people willing to take action and a narrative of future possibilities are still the very backbone of every challenge Denkstatt tackles today. The scheme helps them to navigate between the different demands and to convince pension funds, investors, or municipalities to takeover buildings under 'Baurecht'.

A relational understanding of design

The idea of design in dialogue starts from the strong belief that transformation is a relational reality. After a project has been completed, its larger impact and the significance of its urban design often remain unknown. Its physical form becomes part of the larger collection of objects and constellations that shape a city and get meaning by the way it is used, how it impacts the life of people and evokes reactions. A design process can as such never be detached from the large variety of groups and actors that experience and construct the everyday reality around the same project. Not necessarily because design needs to be a result of its collective vision but because its essence lies in how the designed project or program is used or interpreted by others (and not solely the architect). The design becomes part of a larger puzzle of existing routines, a large variety of stakes or an ever-growing set of differing narratives. The challenge is to find the right position in this overwhelming sea of claims.

This relational approach to urban transformation and design has some clear consequences. It confronts the practice of design with the idea that urban transformation is never fully under control and is constantly changing. Every element of a design process, from the first conceptual sketches to the details of a facade, is as such both a very precise operation and a possibly irrelevant anecdote. This acknowledgment of a process of urban transformation never being completed, inspired all the three offices equally: how can we rethink architectural practice beyond the continuous attempt to match the unique qualities of a building with bold plans of future use(r)s and possible investment schemes? How do we develop the ability to deal with the experimental and long-term character of urban transformations?

04   To prove their point, Denkstatt tested different 1:1 models showing how living and working can be merged at Zentrale Pratteln. Building a community and identity goes hand in hand with questioning the underlying development model of a building.

05   Triggering future expectations activates the demand of alternative use and gives Denkstatt the position to operate.

TID tower

Designed as a monolith, the TID tower avoids the image of the modern glass tower. It starts as an ellipse and ends as a rectangle. The building's simple shape fully captures the Mediterranean light of Tirana (Albania) and generates a wide range of unexpected shadows. It does not symbolize anything, but simply highlights an environmental and, as such, cultural condition.

The TID tower is 51N4E's architectural response to Tirana's urgency to bring the city back into the hearts and minds of the citizens as a collective space. The design and construction of the tower was a cultural adventure. Through collaboration, common references were built and underlying beliefs were questioned. This was not meant as a strategy to open the debate but as a prudent move to collectively learn and mutually share while shaping a common project.

06   A mock-up of the TID tower aiming at convincing and training contractors, developers and administration of the feasibility of the challenging facade structure.

07   The TID tower situated in the city center of Tirana close to Skanderbeg Square.

Moments of closure

The ambitious concept of the TID tower was a challenge for 51N4E as well as for the contractors, local government and developers involved. Such a tower continuously triggers and questions existing practices and demands innovative solutions. This reinterprets one of the central mechanisms of urban transformation: the selectivity ingrained in the system.

Different rules, traditions and procedures secure the preferred direction of urban transformation often safeguarded and strengthened by sets of legal, administrative and even design instruments and professional roles. Overruling such selective mechanisms on a temporary basis creates important room for manoeuvre. Although these windows of opportunities eventually close again, the established old patterns of spatial production sometimes remain slightly changed.

Design in dialogue tries to take back control of this central mechanism of urban transformation by inviting the architect to take up responsibility and to consider a political position that is often inherent. Being a privileged partner in processes of urban transformation, architects and other spatial practitioners are in the perfect position to find ways to change or tackle existing ways of working.

This whole notion of reacting to moments of closure activates the relational understanding of design. Designs, plans, ideas, concepts and even built buildings, however massive or carefully worked out, will always change, and must change in order to survive and to give space to a more open and flexible design attitude. If changes, adaptations, appropriations, corrections and transformations are not understood as mistakes but as a necessary process of becoming, then processes of planning can be seen as dynamic games with open outcomes.

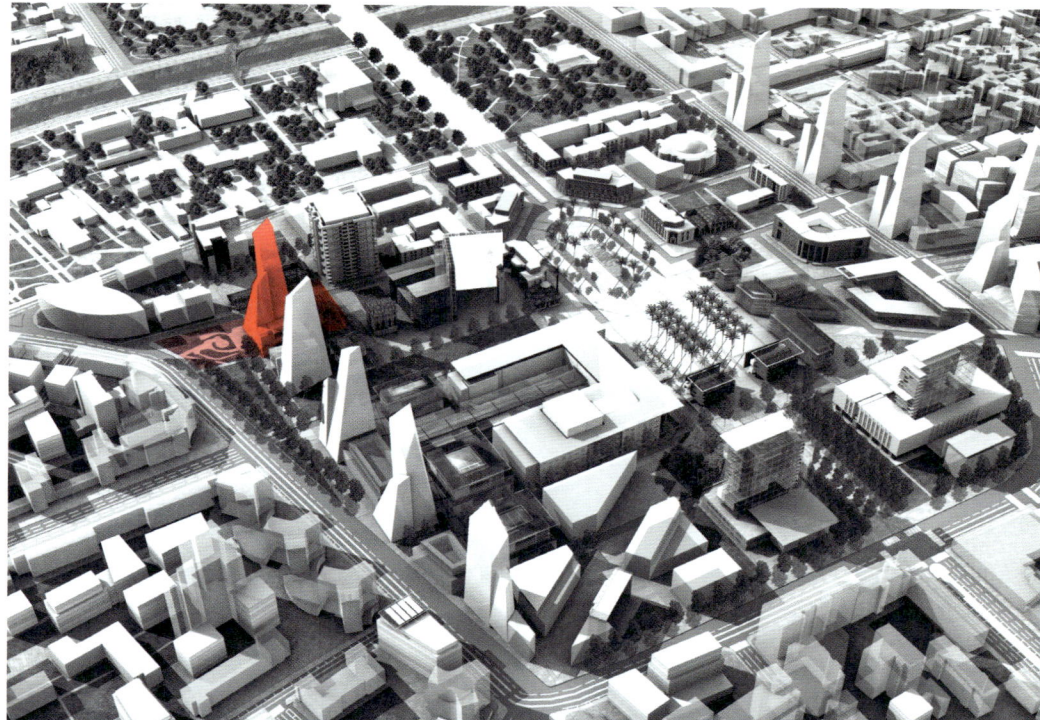

08–09 The TID tower is part of a larger dynamic of changing urban visions. The strategic and symbolic character of the project urges for careful experimentation.

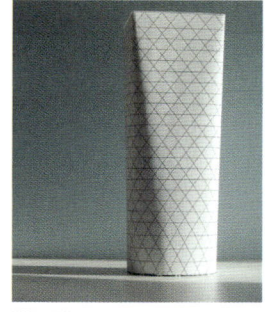

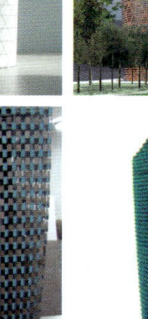

Prudent moves

Even though the design of TID tower and the slow reconversion of Zentrale Pratteln are completely different projects, they both created the necessary room for manoeuvre through bold and prudent moves. While the experimental character of the design of the TID tower and the long-term process of negotiation created the conditions to collectively rethink the approach to urban transformation, the introduction of new actors and intermediate users, in the case of Zentrale Pratteln, created the space to experiment and to show the necessity to develop differently.

10-17 A series of studies on the facade of the TID tower as different attempts to make the most out of the possibilities of the current situation and to create a certain sense of understanding and care.

The selectivity of urban transformation can best be challenged by revealing the complexity of the everyday and by exposing underlying, highly diverse interpretations of reality.

Often, we are unaware of how selective our observations are, how procedures and design briefs already are themselves specific interpretations of a complex and ever-changing reality. Including new voices can help to overcome this problem. They have a crucial and liberating role to play. By mapping the complexity of reality, dominant discourses, which far too often are presented as absolute truths, can be challenged. Revealing alternative interpretations paves new paths and creates the mental space to explore new possibilities.

Embracing the idea of the city as an immense collection of data, artefacts, experiences and skills is a prerequisite for a multifaceted understanding of urban reality and urban transformation. The facade of a house, the way we use a square or the personal description of a neighborhood or a street, all give us insights into the different and personal ways we read and understand our (un)built environment. Often, a small part of this data and a minority of perspectives are used and activated within a design project only. If you start to reject this undetailed, selective and unnuanced reading of reality, a new context for architectural practice emerges.

Introducing new perspectives is not always comfortable. Activating everyday knowledge is a very vulnerable process and a highly political act. New perspectives highlight inequalities, restrictions, or contradictions. It brings new actors to the table, which might feel as a threat to those who hold power. This disruptive moment needs guidance to be productive. It is necessary to carve out paths that create the possibility to deconstruct existing interpretations and to develop new shared ground for design and creativity.

From this perspective design in dialogue could be seen as a craft. A craft that uses the momentum of engagement to realize a process of collective interpretation and an informed discussion. That, in turn, can lead to new solutions—solutions that might lead beyond the boundaries of what is commonly accepted.

2

Knowledge of the many

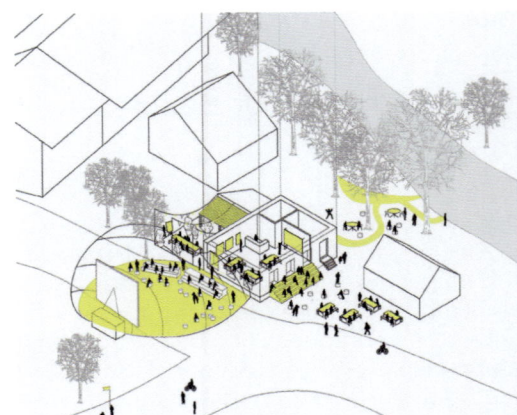

18   A first test of how to transform an existing abandoned building into a place of gathering to create awareness around Studio Dietikon.

Studio Dietikon

Launched in 2018, Denkstatt started to collaborate with the town planning office of Dietikon (Switzerland) to organize a new interface between citizens, city administration and politics. Located in the old offices of the Building Authority, Studio Dietikon hosts events and workshops to create opportunities for encounters and exchanges.

The understanding of design in dialogue in Studio Dietikon directly emerges from a strong belief in discussion and mutual listening as a mode of collaboration and action. This position is directly reflected in the methodology of Studio Dietikon, creating a seemingly endless series of settings to discuss the past and future of the city: from a mobile coffee corner, a hyperlocal cinema to temporary interventions in public and private spaces. With its focus on local narratives and the activation of a local community, Studio Dietikon literally translates the second dimension of design in dialogue 'knowledge of the many' into different physical settings for research and action. The persistence of the Denkstatt team to continuously invent and build new environments for debate, forms the basis of the success of this project. Aware of the highly political context of their operation, Denkstatt achieved to create a kind of parallel universe and a way of working that allowed to hover between the territory and the map, the plan and reality, the citizens and its city administration.

19   A stove as the "first element" of Denkstatt's architecture of dialogue.

20   The old offices of the Building Authority of Dietikon became the basecamp of the whole operation. With a mobile workshop structure, Studio Dietikon visited neighborhoods to discuss the present and future of this small town near Zurich.

for alternative models of transformation (as illustrated under dimension 4–6 in this book) design in dialogue tries to create the right conditions for meaningful conversations and as such actively deals with (finding alternatives for) the everlasting struggle for power and influence.

From knowledge to action

The collective nature of the work of Denkstatt in Studio Dietikon highlights how design in dialogue differentiates itself from a more classical understanding of field research in architectural practice. In most cases, a period of careful observation and thorough analysis plays a key role in defining possible future interventions, the program of a project or the reinterpretation of a project brief. Design in dialogue tries to take this already established logic of research and analysis a step further by transforming it towards a collective moment of interpretation.

This is done by firstly creating a kind of common ground: a rich and diverse reading of reality, revealing existing phenomena and unravelling complexity by presenting rough observations, excerpts of interviews and (spatial) data. In a second step this collection of knowledge is used to carefully position the different actors at stake (and by inviting previously neglected stakeholders to join the table). By collectively tracing differences, opportunities and gaps, the data forms the ideal mirror to specify the common aspirations of a project and potential points of friction. Organizing this moment of collective interpretation around actual data and observations helps to preserve existing ideological positions or power differences from dominating the debate.

Changing patterns of democracy

Power and inequality are inherent to design in dialogue. Some coalition members will need to be strengthened to enable their active participation in a shared process, while others, having the tendency to appropriate the space and freedom within a process primarily to defend their own interests, will need to learn how to open up. Design in dialogue is therefore not only a question of organizing a shared process, but also of supporting specific groups to become part of the conversation and of creating the room for a variety of (opposing) interests to clash or change. The designer, but also the civil servant, the agitator, the expert civilian, the developer, the researcher, the politician, all have their role to play. Becoming aware of the strengths and weaknesses of the different positions and their possible combinations is key.

For projects such as Studio Dietikon, this understanding is extremely important in order to avoid becoming delusional or overly naïve. The ideal situation or argument-based deliberation that lies at the basis of design in dialogue must be complemented with a more disruptive or agonistic understanding of democratic practices. By activating moments of friction or campaigning

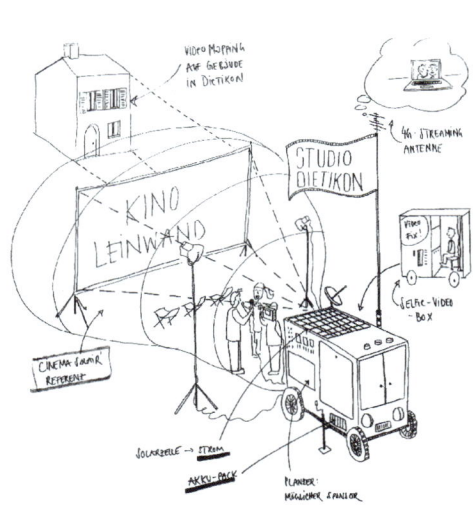

21   A first sketch of the technical device Denkstatt wanted to develop for Studio Dietikon. By listening, observing and making a documentary they tried to find niches, blind spots or open doors that allowed them to move and act in (un)known territories.

22   After three months of interviewing the citizens of Dietikon, the resulting documentary was screened. In a first moment of collective reflection, people started listening to each other. Based on the documentary, a larger debate on the possible futures of Dietikon started and first interventions were tested.

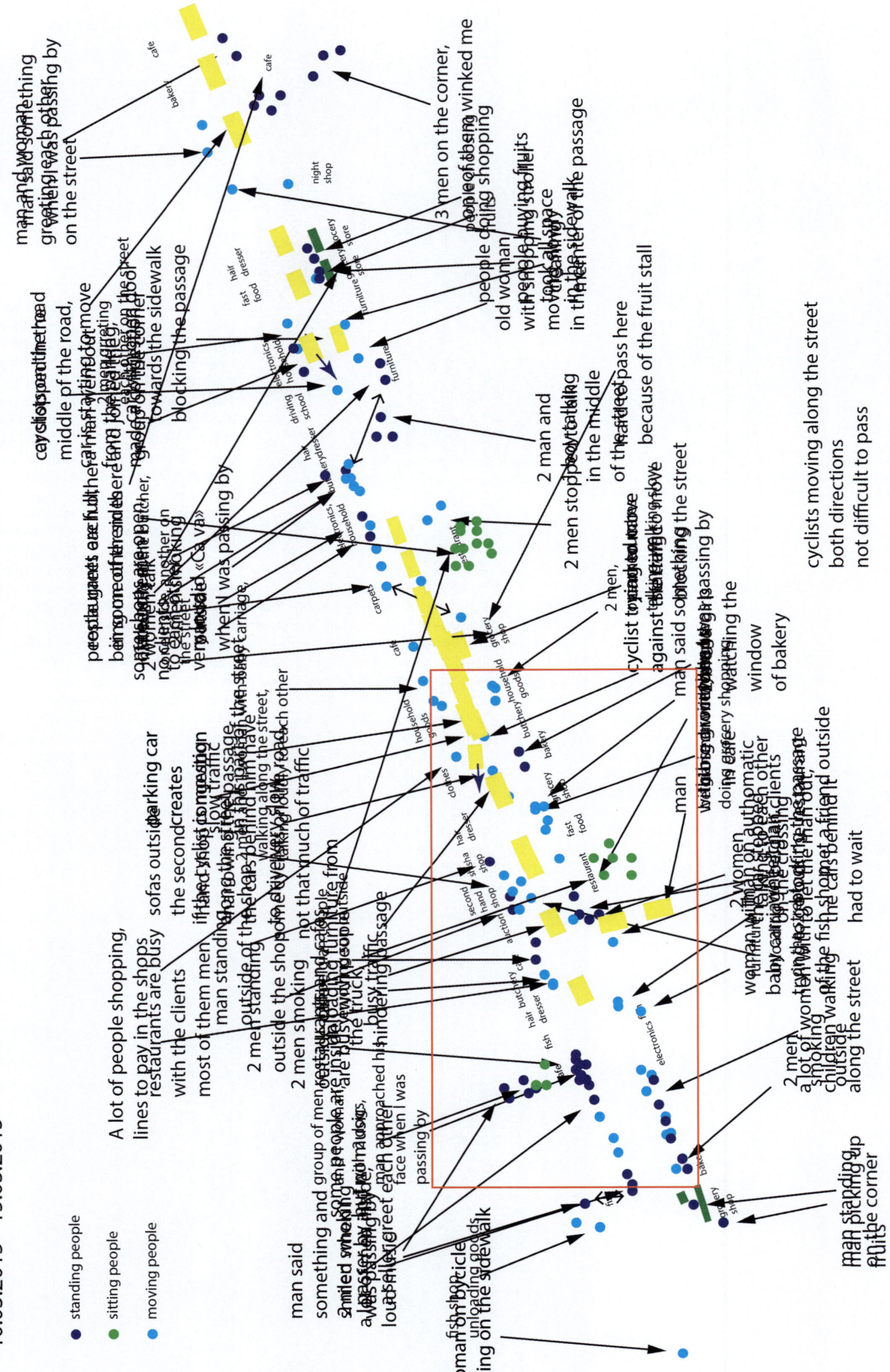

10.03.2015 – 15.03.2015

- standing people
- sitting people
- moving people

30

23   By observing the street in different moments in time, Endeavour gained an overview of uses that could later be brought into the discussion.

Handelsstraat

In 2014 the city of Antwerp (Belgium) asked Endeavour to come up with a method to include the perception of safety in the city's design and program guidelines for the public domain. Endeavour quickly chose to not develop 'checklists' or ready-made design solutions, but to instead work on manuals of reading and activating space within the municipal workflow, developed and tested through case-studies. The strategic ambition of this type of output was to open up and re-think standardized procedures, emphasizing the importance of mobilizing different types of knowledge already embedded within the cities administration but divided over different policy domains.

One of the four manuals, 'The Phenomena-Map', describes common patterns of use and social interactions that can be used as a common framework to discuss the possible overlap of spatial claims. The manual describes four subsequent stages to operationalize this approach: observations by the researchers to identify socio-spatial 'phenomena', translation of these observations into an illustrative map or 'phenomena-atlas', individual, in-depth interviews with key actors to interpret the map and finally a workshop bringing all the interviewed actors around the table.

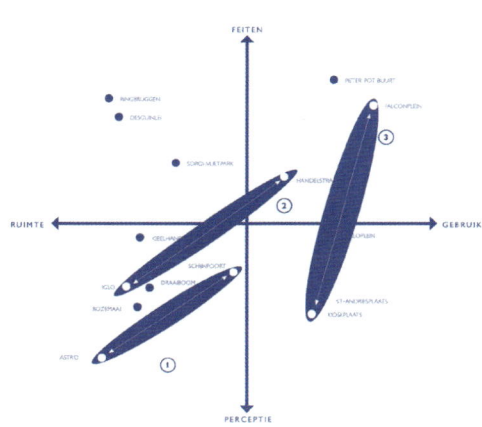

24   Based on individual interviews with the police, shop owners and inhabitants of the street, Endeavour added a subjective layer to the illustrated observations. The different positions were made place-specific, enabling the collective evaluation and questioning of them.

25   A first categorization of safety and public space in Antwerp. What are the cases with an actual safety problem? Where does perception play a role? The overview of cases created a shared starting point between Endeavour and the respectively responsible city administrations to explore underlying dynamics.

26   Different perceptions on the use of the street dominated the debate for years. By allocating these positions to specific users and phenomena, Endeavour tried to create a framework for negotiation.

27   A photo of the final discussion with some users of the street. The map with phenomena and subjective positions of each of the participants proved to create enough shared ground to enter the sensitive discussion under which conditions certain uses are desirable or not.

Redingenhof

In a small street near a school in Leuven (Belgium), a group of inhabitants with the support of 51N4E and Plant & Houtgoed decided to organize an experiment to naturalize their street and the surrounding private and public properties. This experiment, part of a larger campaign of the Flemish Government, became an interesting test ground for combining technical, design based and process-oriented approaches to rethink the existing culture and practices of land use in Flanders.

The project of Redingenhof started with drafting an ambition matrix. Through dialogue, this form became a shared framework where objectives, dreams and tensions were made explicit. Continuously challenged by the strategy of temporary mock-ups, central to the work of 51N4E, the grid served as a tool for evaluation, allowing to test new insights and a prioritization of projects based on the ambitions that were put to the fore.

Activating design in dialogue through the organization of mock-ups and interventions seems to be an interesting but challenging method. The direct impact of certain design decisions evoked fierce reactions (both positive and negative). It continuously challenged the group to take a position (Can we question the existing legal framework?) and to develop methodologies to organize themselves (How do we make decisions? With whom do we collaborate?). As such, the project of Redingenhof combines the work of the Handelsstraat and Studio Dietikon. It develops tools to translate knowledge into action while actively manoeuvring through multiple scales.

28   A collective dinner with the inhabitants of the street as an important moment to experience the qualities of the naturalization of their street and to collectively discuss, reflect and celebrate the ongoing collective action (and learning).

29–30   Two alternative proposals for the naturalization of the street. The uneven impact on parking space becomes a topic of debate.

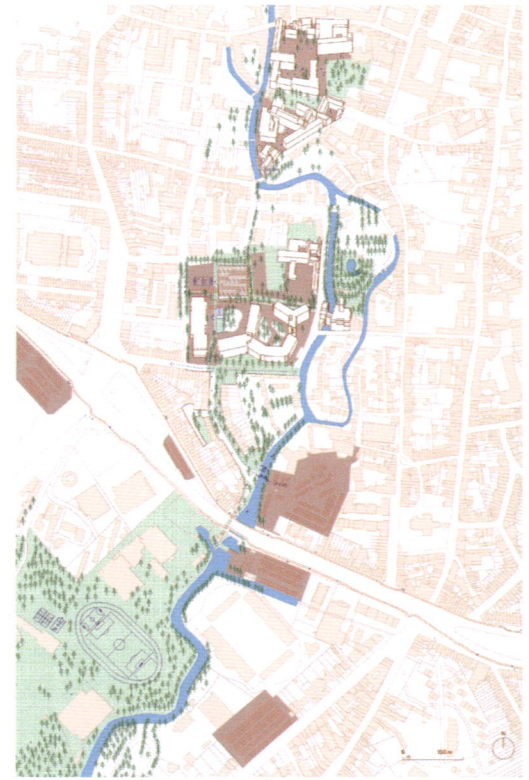

31   A map showing the water and natural structures around the street, framing Redingenhof as an important link in a broader network. This drawing helped to set the ambitions and invite other stakeholders around the table.

32   Before intervening, a mock-up was created together with the inhabitants to discuss and negotiate the upcoming intervention.

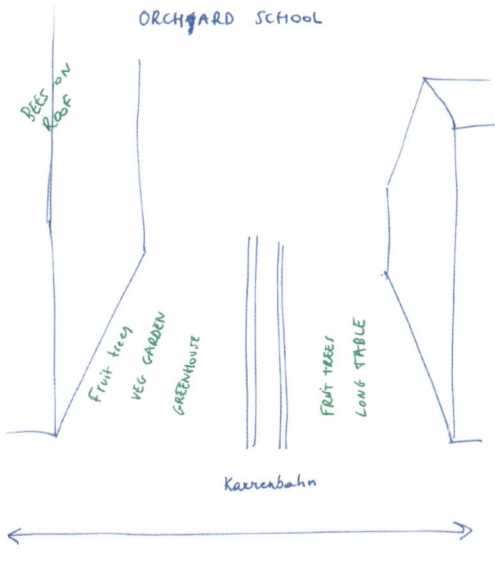

33   A sketch on the new profile of the street near the school. Introducing new types of vegetation, a greenhouse and a bee-friendly environment.

34   A quick sketch to adapt and rethink the proposed design. Drawing in a direct and light way became an important tool to discuss the consequences of certain proposals and collectively think of alternative scenarios.

The reinterpretation of knowledge

The challenging set-up of the Redingenhof project sheds new light on how to (re)interpret knowledge. The collective nature of the endeavor is complemented with the need to develop a shared practice of organizing and discussing social-spatial research. Through an iterative cycle of identifying questions, testing out strategies, gathering insights and collectively evaluating the action, a shared reflexive attitude is developed that allows the group to deal with possible internal contradictions. The methodology of introducing mock-ups to test possible interventions challenges both, the object and the subject of the action: the way the group and space is organized.

Dealing with this double dynamic requires specific methodologies and tools that help to dissolve the barrier between researcher and participant. In a common mode of exploration, new areas for investigation, niches or blind spots are traced to help a group engaging with (un)known territories.

35–37   After realizing a first mock-up of the redesigned street, some latent differences came to the surface. The tangibility of the mock-up accelerated the dialogue process, which had already been going on for six months, and threatened to divide neighbors into camps of supporters and opponents. In the subsequent meeting, both camps asked not to continue the project if these conflicts persisted. Votes were even raised for a trajectory without participation, to avoid discussion. Given that the opponents are a very small minority, this event raised questions on how to develop a shared understanding of the trajectory that was collectively designed. When does a co-creative project have sufficient support? Does everyone have to agree? Who will be involved in the dialogue? Which rituals do we introduce to guide collective reflection?

3

Safe ground for learning

Curiosity towards the unknown

A mode of collective exploration as presented in Dietikon, Handelsstraat and Redingenhof engages with a wide variety of ways of reading and understanding reality. It is this multitude of memories and experiences that creates the organic and layered nature of space. Working towards a more social and sustainable form of design and urban development requires looking at architecture and urban design not only as a technical or expert-driven profession focused on excellence, but also as a discipline of engagement focused on inclusion. It is about sharpening the understanding and creating a vocabulary of the situation one is in and about looking for ways to understand the action and the position one can take.

Project ontharding Redingenhof — juli 8/14.
Aantal wagens geparkeerd in de Volmolenlaan.

Datum	Uur	Nrs 2 tot 6	Nrs 8 tot 32	Nr 34 en pleintje rond de elk	Pijpekop (pleintje tussen nrs 6 en 8)	Aantal wagens op de opritten (oneven nrs)
8-7-2019 maandag	10 uur	1	3	4	3	5
	21 uur	5	9	3	3	8
Di. 9/7/19	10 uur	3	3	3	2	2
	21 uur 8u 30	7	6	2	2	6
woe 10/7/19	10 uur	2	3	2	1	4
	21 uur	7	6	4	1	7
Do. 11/7	10 uur	4	5	2	2	3
	21 uur					
Vrij 12/7	10 uur 11u	3	4	2	1	6
	21 uur 23 u	7	8	3	1	6
zat 13/7	10 uur 11	6	7	3	3	7
	21 uur 23 u	5	4	3	3	6
zondag 14/7	10 uur 8	6	7	2	2	8
	21 uur	8	3	2	2	6
	10 uur					
	21 uur					
	10 uur					
	21 uur					
	10 uur					
	21 uur					

38 In order to create enough trust to change the design of the street, 51N4E needed a clear understanding of how the space is used today. By organising a classical parking survey in a co-productive way, enough common ground could be created to have a meaningful discussion on this sensitive matter.

When you acknowledge the strategic nature of a design intervention and its capacity to mediate, recognize or challenge existing practices, you try to carefully situate moments of design in longer trajectories of transformation. The design as such becomes the accumulation of what you think the collectively shared agenda and strategic opportunities of a place could be for a specific moment in time and how this can create the space and rhythm for others to engage.

This is a double movement of proposing new conditions and inviting others to respond, challenges the way we represent architectural practice. A design in dialogue approach does not benefit from the classical emphasis on exclusivity or authorship, which has the tendency to disregard the possibility of contextual changes.

Accepting the idea that each step of a design process can—from the moment it exists—be renegotiated, needs a language and a design attitude that reveals in a direct, explicit and uncompromising way the implications of the design and the possibilities to reconfigure it.

It means you accept that design is never a result or an object with a clearly defined finality, but always the impetus for something new. Limiting yourself to a linear representation of what is, after all, a creative pattern of design in action, does not make sense. Instead, the art of testing, mediating, choosing position and initiating changes, results in a process that can be considered as a constant iteration of smaller sprints. It gets rid of a predefined form or function of the output of a design process.

Creating the right moment for collaboration and the experience to collectively reinterpret reality becomes the core creative act of this process. Rather than reducing design in dialogue to the field of participation or a particular phase in a design process, it could be considered as a way to navigate the whole technical and political field of urban transformation.

A moment of design thus becomes the necessary safe ground for learning: a setting that helps to collectively challenge existing patterns of urban transformation and allows for uncertainty, amateurism or slowness. Then, and only then, will we develop a capacity to adapt to ever-changing conditions by designing leeway improvements on the fly.

39   A site visit of the Dry Docks, getting to know all the technical details of how a dock works and what would need to be restored to make them fully operational.

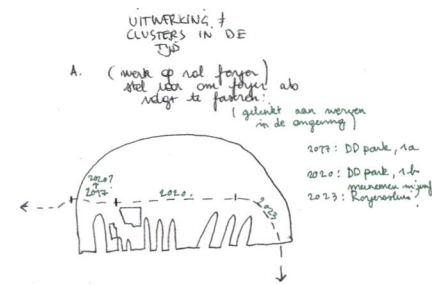

41   Dealing with the complexity of the Dry Docks needed a strategy to integrate different scales and physical and organizational dynamics. This resulted in a spatial framework that deconstructed the site in smaller bits and pieces, supporting different types of ownership while gradually building up towards a larger narrative of reintroducing productive activities in the city.

Translation and narration

The design of the different instruments activated in the Dry Docks projects were all based on finding formats to make existing conflicts explicit, always within the rhythm of a safe conversation. Combining all claims of future users challenged the way the city was managing the site and questioned the financialization or market-led development of the site. 51N4E and Endeavour were challenged to properly assess positions and interests and to come up with the right (visual) language to respond. What type of image, what form of output, what kind of narrative, appeals to which sensitivities or interests? And how can a succession of presentations, confrontations or interpretations create a process that invites you to question certain things and create the space for imagination and negotiation? Translation and narration are as such not only about phrasing it well, but also about sensing and reacting to the interest of others and their ability and position to intervene and, again, change the order of things.

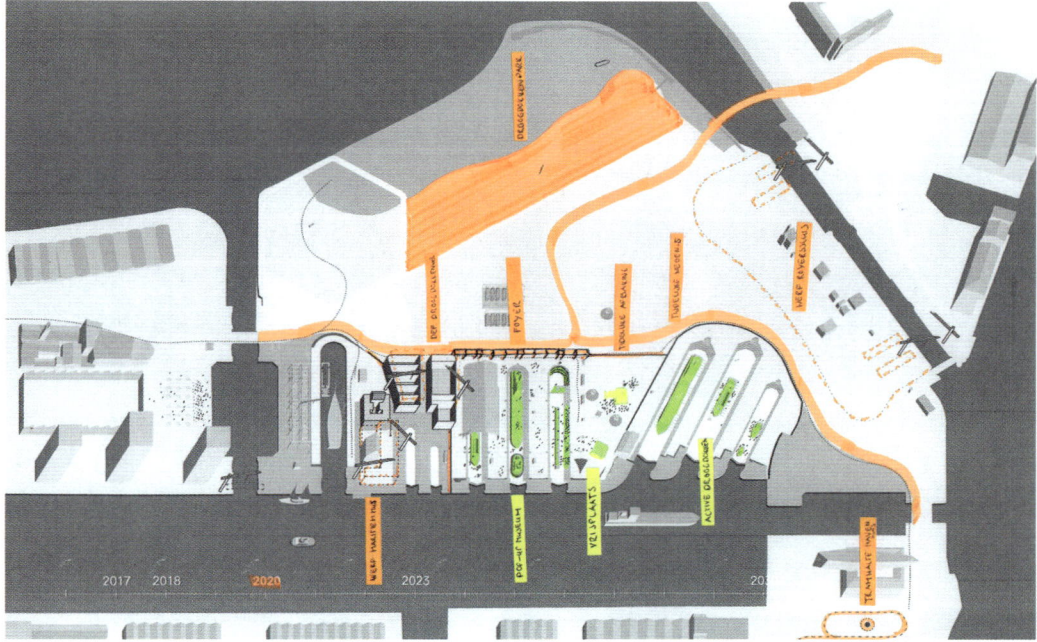

40   The time dimension of the redevelopment of the Dry Docks urged 51N4E and Endeavour to experiment with new representations for the masterplan, focussed on the relationship between things, rather than things themselves.

Dry Docks in Antwerp

Over the years, the Dry Docks of Antwerp (Belgium) lost their economic function and were about to become a future void in the city. In collaboration with 51N4E, Endeavour was asked to respond to this new situation and develop a strategy to activate the site. A future exhibition space of maritime heritage needed to be combined with a productive spot for local economy and craftsmanship while preserving the freedom and experimental qualities of this urban no-man's-land.

Building a vision for such a new part of the city cannot depend on a masterplan alone, but requires a group of future users to contribute to the project from the start. This challenged 51N4E and Endeavour to redesign the instruments of a masterplanning process.

The work started with a structured and broad process of understanding all the different positions at stake and the various technical consequences and spatial implications of a long list of possible future activities. This was translated in a charter that set the collective ambitions of all future users, and a manual that described all the possible questions that could arise during the transformation of the site. The spatial interventions that supported the charter and manual were understood as a series of new settings that step-by-step reframed the existing condition. They were designed to introduce new spatial configurations and uses and to challenge existing ownership in order to form the basis for a new host community for this, at the start, almost forgotten part of Antwerp.

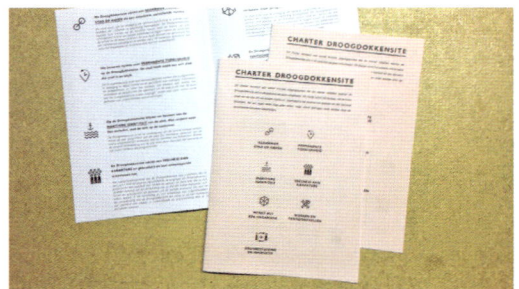

42   An important part of redeveloping the Dry Docks was to create a new coalition between economic, cultural and civic actors. The charter became a key tool to define main strands and keep the focus.

43   The existing two-meter-wide walls constrained possible transformations of Alvéoles Saint-Nazaire.

Alvéoles
Saint Nazaire

During the Second World War, a huge submarine base was built by the occupying forces in the city of Saint Nazaire on the French Atlantic coast. When the city was flattened towards the end of the war, the base was the only building left standing. Some twenty years ago, the city started to appropriate the building, turning its awkwardness into its main asset.

When confronted with the question of relocating the popular Jaques Brel Hall inside the submarine basis, the time was right to re-evaluate the functioning of the whole and to tie everything together.

The result is a deliberately simple project that puts the emphasis more on the urban district than on the particular building: an infrastructure activating a broad range of possibilities for various future users. The architecture of the project is basic and yet offers a strong physical impact: referring to the context of the bunker and of the water, the architecture is not only to be admired, but first of all to be used intensely as part of the everyday life of the city.

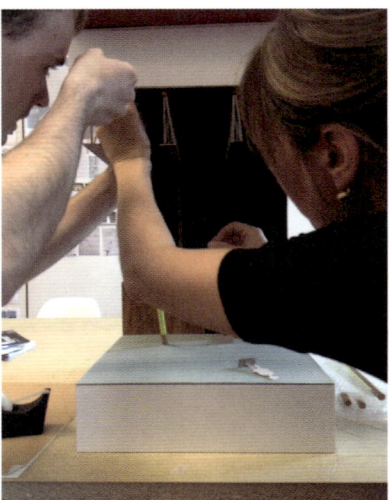

44   A scenographic model of the design as an invitation to discuss different possibilities.

Tacit technicity

In both projects, the double meaning of experience played out. Even without having tangible or recognized experience in a specific field, it is meaningful for everyone involved to go through the experience and learn from it, experts and beginners alike. For all stakeholders involved, the project raised new questions and challenged them to shift positions. This condition where nobody completely knows how to do it, creates a collective learning experience of managing the instability that is inherent in any transformation process. In these circumstances it becomes important to constantly look for new forms to reframe, remediate, or reconcile possible conflicts and integrate different modes of argumentation. In these situations, it is the tacit technicity of the stakeholders that leads the dance.

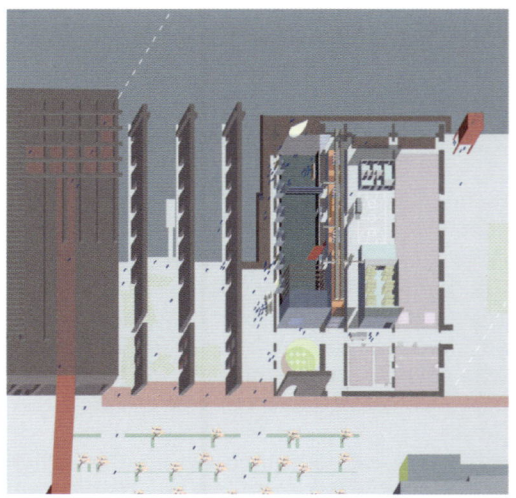

45   A detail of the urban reality drawing of Alvéoles Saint Nazaire. The urban reality drawing articulates the setting in which the project intervenes, with its specific narratives and dynamics. It shows how the project absorbs and activates the context and thus evolves over time, through design research and dialogues with a diversity of parties.

Communicating design

In design in dialogue the language of design becomes something that triggers imagination and leaves room for others to respond, question or add to what is proposed. This double logic is intrinsic to all the different interventions of a design in dialogue approach: from the drawings that are presented, the mock-ups that are tested, to the context (questions, roles, perspectives) that is created around an intervention. From a design in dialogue point of view, an intervention cannot solely be evaluated by its form. Instead, its capacity to introduce a new culture of spatial production and its ability to act as a reference for future actions becomes key. This completely shifts the position of the designer.

In order to cherish the vulnerability of first ideas and to allow conflict to exist, waiting, leaving room for collective reflection, or proactive engagement, are just as important as creativity, excellence or hard work.

47   The introduction of an overscaled light fixture stressed the public importance of the route along the water.

46   A model of Alvéoles Saint Nazaire. Through its materiality and color, the model shows a difference between what is fixed, or a given and what is open for dialogue.

a model of testing new configurations to incrementally find common ground and unravel how existing or future infrastructure can have a bigger capacity to adapt in the long run. The dialogue around these processes clearly starts from a relational perspective. It is more focused on the relationship between timeframes and objects than on the negotiation or the approval of the design itself. In Alvéoles Saint-Nazaire, the urban reality drawing and its ability to situate interventions in their larger whole, played an important role to facilitate this conversation. For the Dry docks in Antwerp, on the other hand, it was the common framework and the detailed inventory of conditions and possibilities that were the tools to introduce a relational mode of thinking.

48   The cabinet de curiosités as a tangible way to discuss the relationship between frame (the base) and infill (the different interventions).

Adaptive infrastructure

In both the Alvéoles Saint-Nazaire and the Dry Docks project, the existing buildings and infrastructure defined the conditions. The clear limits and specific use of the maritime heritage sites were challenged by an increasing number of urban schemes that were projected throughout the years. These new combinations of future living environments and infrastructural heritage need a design approach that engages with the complex and temporal process of urban transformation. Neither the concrete two-meter-wide walls and ten-meter-deep ceiling in Alvéoles Saint-Nazaire nor the twenty-meter-wide and seven-meter-high dry docks in Antwerp are physical qualities that are easy to transform. Adapting these infrastructures needs an intervention method that starts from possible future users and includes new governance and financial models in the design exercise. It needs

49   Alvéoles Saint Nazaire during a regular bingo evening.

Collective learning and action

Design in dialogue starts from an ethos of radical openness, a practice that creates new conditions and gives others the possibility to add, remove or change its meaning and significance. Often focused on trajectories of collective learning and action, design in dialogue creates the possibility to collectively redefine the expectations and limits of urban transformation. A collective learning trajectory can be defined as: the recurrent process during which a (changing) group of people actively and collectively tries to (re)define and test how, why, what and in relation to whom they are organizing themselves.

It is through these collective reflections that moments of opportunities for action are defined. Understanding and identifying multiple ways to intervene is the result and not the precondition of collaboration. It is only by understanding the interdependencies between different actors that the opportunities and constraints of bigger institutional structures become visible.

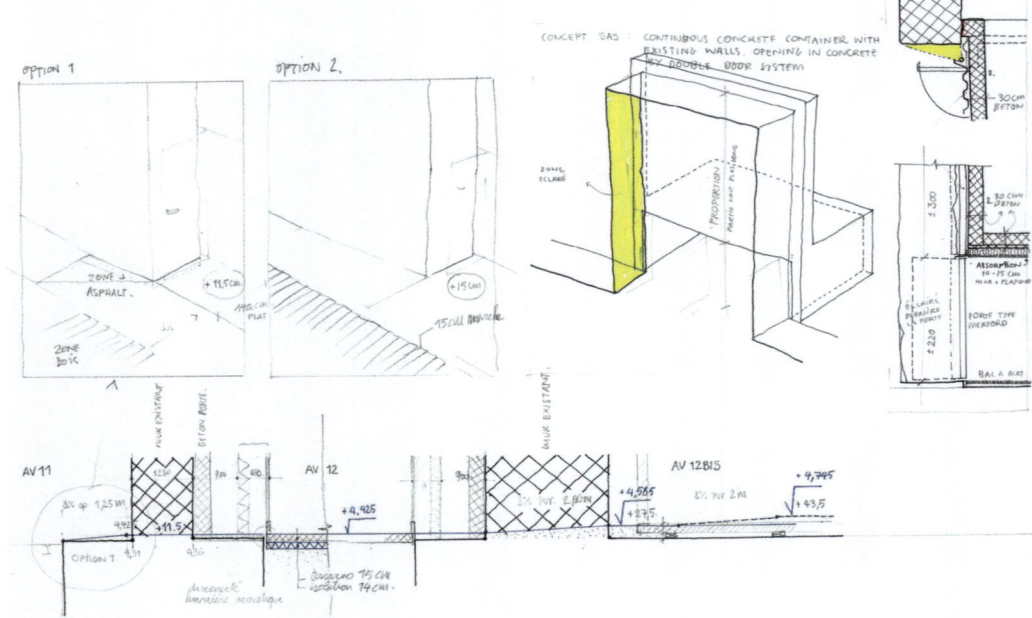

50   The dialogue process created the shift from having only one to having multiple entrances, detailed as transition spaces occupying the thickness of the existing walls.

51   On-site discussion on material choices. The urban reality drawing of Alvéoles Saint Nazaire hanging on the wall.

52   Discussing the materiality of the intervention. Finding formats to discuss future choices becomes key in all the different scales of the architectural project.

53   Overview of the Alvéoles Saint Nazaire, with the project appearing as a series of interventions.

4

Risky experiments

Urban designers and architects can try to mediate between different interests, but they do not always have enough leverage to initiate vulnerable and non-mainstream approaches. When market mechanisms of urban transformation and spatial production, become dominant, like standardized typologies of housing or participatory trajectories with a single focus on avoiding conflict, new practices will no longer occur. Far too often, projects that renounce standard solutions or risk-avoiding strategies get bogged down.

The introduction of vulnerable claims on different scales or alternative agendas for urban transformation, such as adaptive re-use or cooperative ownership structures, need a more disruptive approach to claim their space around the table. Economic interests and a high investment pressure often lead to risk aversion among developers or owners. Usually, they are not too keen on experimenting let alone on including a social innovative approach.

In these cases, the first three dimensions of design in dialogue (out of necessity, knowledge of the many, safe ground for learning) do not suffice. Questioning existing coalitions and modes of working by revealing unheard voices will not create enough discomfort to rethink current practices, nor will specific settings of safe ground for learning trigger enough to fundamentally question underlying mechanisms and patterns of spatial production. These kinds of situations require a more entrepreneurial and confrontational behavior. Design in dialogue becomes the practice of developing and testing unconventional possibilities to engage with a topic, a precise site or a larger project. By taking the critical ethos of architectural practice as a leading example, it is about inventing new means of communication, new operational structures or simply daring bold actions.

If you want to break away from a situation of stagnation, it is necessary to launch radical, refreshing ideas and initiatives yourself. Questioning a certain development model is then no longer sufficient. You have to set up parts of the transformation, invest in temporary implementations, enter into alliances with new groups of users that require other development models and increasingly take on a combination of different roles at the same time: from designer, to user, financial manager and expert.

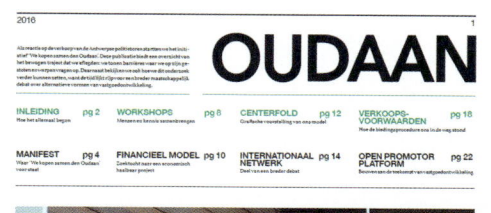

54 A newspaper promoting the cooperative model for the Oudaan.

We kopen samen den Oudaan

The Oudaan is a city icon of Antwerp (Belgium) dividing opinions for decades. Designed by the modernist architect Renaat Braem, the Oudaan was supposed to become part of the civic core of the city transforming Antwerp's skyline. Next to the 'Boerentoren', representing the city's economic significance, and the Cathedral of Our Lady Mary, Antwerp's symbol of religious devotion, Braem envisioned the Oudaan as a sign for civic pride and a model of efficient serviceability, indicating the dawning of the modern era.

On June 27, 2015, AG Vespa (the city of Antwerp's autonomous real estate company) officially declared the tower for sale. On that same evening, Endeavour launched an impulsive call to buy the Oudaan together via social media. The campaign 'We kopen samen den Oudaan' started to trigger the debate around the social and sustainable significance of monumental real estate in the city and illustrated the large variety of roles architecture could play to support this collective claim.

55 A detail of the interior of the Oudaan, exhibited during the campaign to create awareness around the civic value of the building.

Changing, translating and building new relations for action

When you engage with this more radical interpretation of design in dialogue, you need to engage with a large variety of other fields to fully grasp and operationalize the whole complexity of a new urban practice. Financial expertise, communication skills, programming and governance become increasingly important to develop an own approach and to be taken serious by others.

The possibility to shift in professional roles not only creates the opportunity to practice through experience, but also creates a certain clarity on the collective nature of future actions. Finding freedoms through risky experiments structurally establishes a collective mode of working. The professional and voluntary way of communicating in the 'We kopen samen den Oudaan' project allowed others to be surprised. People started to engage in this initiative to test previously undiscovered futures, and rethink their own position in the light of action.

57 A render of a possible space in the Oudaan made for a campaign to find possible tenants and create traction for the potential of the conversion of use.

Collective ownership

Strict regulations or predefined logics often drastically reduce the possibilities of spatial transformation due to given ownership structures. Rethinking the latter becomes a key reason to engage with risky experiments and find new freedom for action. Specific modes of collaboration and action can trigger the status quo of real estate development. More specifically even, these processes of innovation can change the rules of the game to a more shared and public model of development. In its most radical way, this leads to newly established collective ownership models that involve non-profit or charitable owners during the transformation process. This was tested in 'We kopen samen den Oudaan' and successfully implemented in the project of Gundeldinger Feld. More and more often new logics and time frames that challenge the internal logics of existing real estate models are introduced and tested. This is also the case for the WTC project presented under the following two dimensions of design in dialogue (senior improvisor and culture of cooperation).

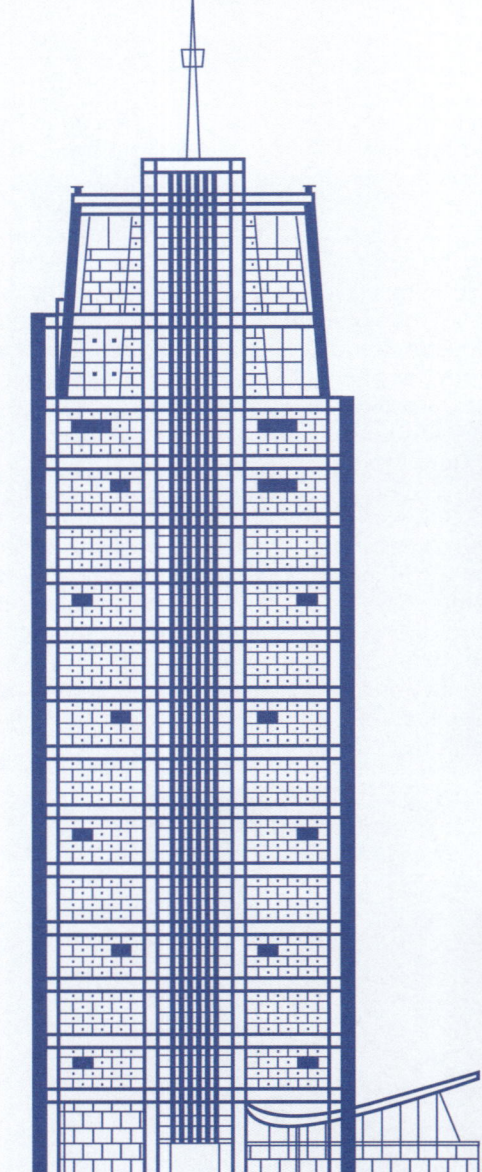

56 A first attempt to make a logo for 'We kopen samen den Oudaan'.

58 Exhibiting the concept got people intrigued by the idea. It turned out that a lot of local business owners and organizations were interested in creating a shared space in the heart of the city.

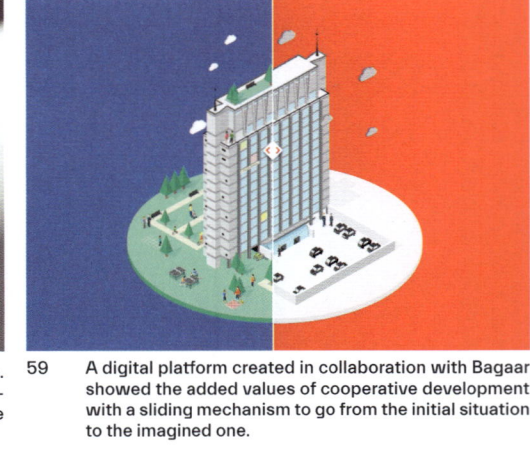

59 A digital platform created in collaboration with Bagaar showed the added values of cooperative development with a sliding mechanism to go from the initial situation to the imagined one.

60 One of the many workshops that were organized to collectively design a more cooperative development model.

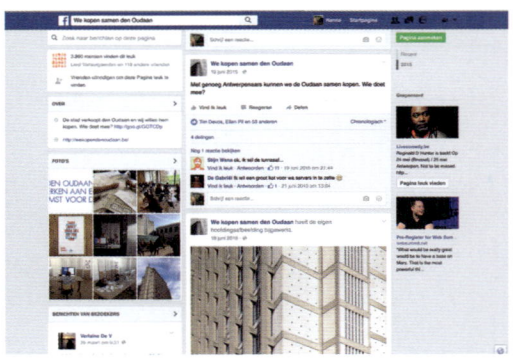

61 The success of the facebook page of the campaing triggered Endeavour to take their initial actions seriously.

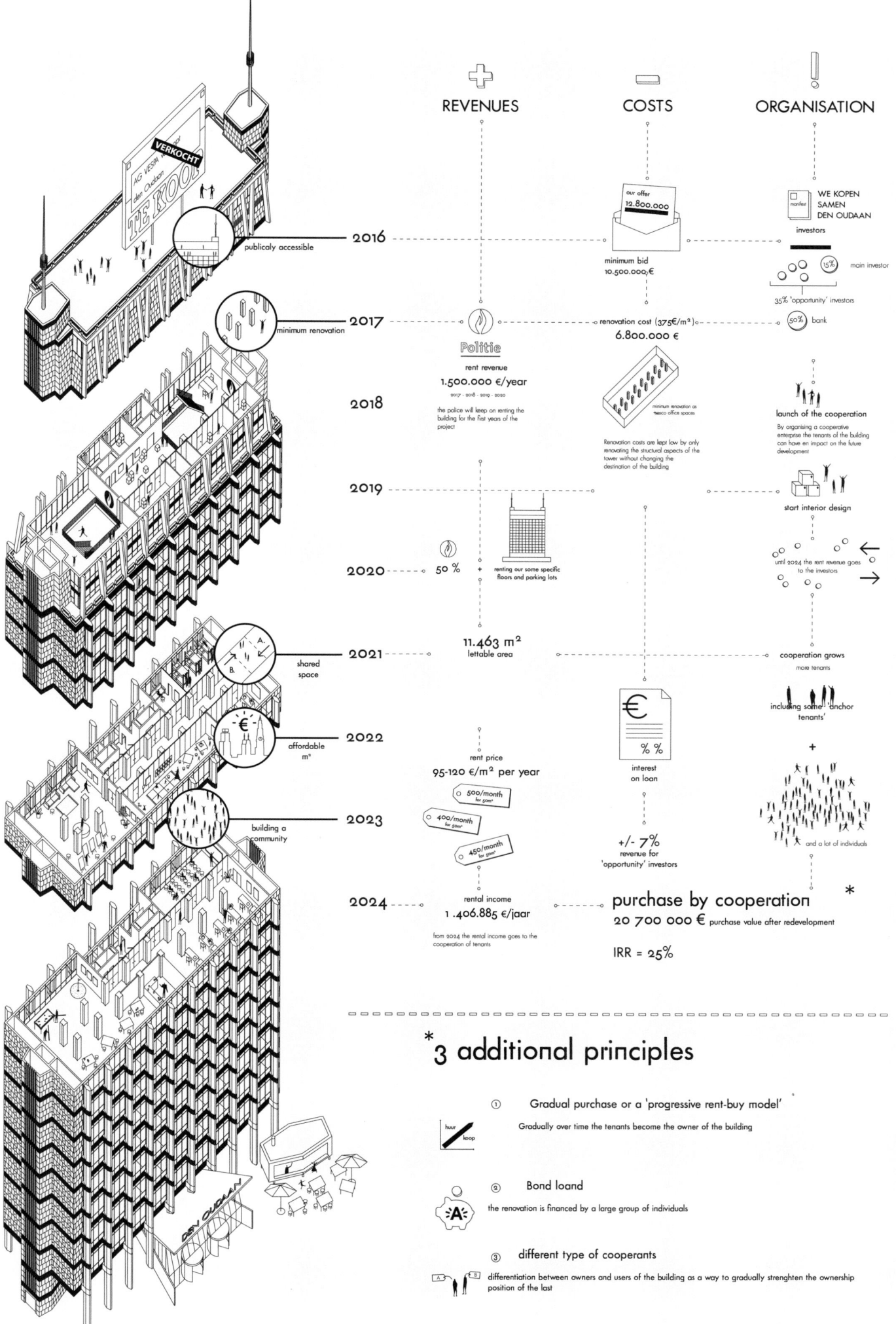

A representation of the financial model of the building showing how a strategy of adaptive reuse could create opportunities for organizations and citizens to become shareholders of this new collective endeavor.

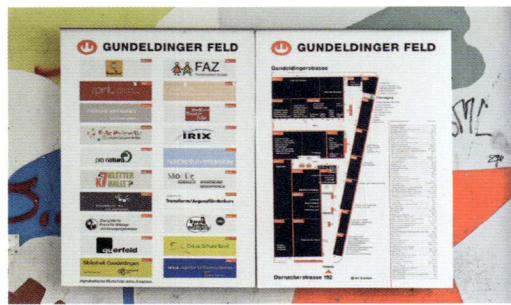

63 An overview of the different organizations that are part of Gundeldinger Feld. From a circus school, climbing wall and carpenter workspace to a library.

64 During the last twenty years Gundeldinger Feld has become a place to experiment with new forms of city making and an example for future neighborhood redevelopment in the city of Basel.

Gundeldinger Feld

It was almost twenty years ago that a group of young architects (later founders of architectural practices such as Baubüro in situ and Denkstatt) and civil actors started to dream about a new future for the Sulzer-Burckhardt machine factory in the Gundeldingen district of Basel (Switzerland). Today the place has become the new living room of the neighborhood and the city, housing over a hundred different types of uses with several hundred visitors per day, taking full advantage of the 1.2 ha site site near Basel train station.

Without project funding or a commission to start with, this project seemed destined to fail. Armed with a fax machine as, at that time, the most important medium for dialogue and a call for ideas to develop a new story for Gundeldingen Feld, the initiators of the project were able to slowly build and proof a new future for the site. They did not do this on their own, but through the involvement of many other companions, a strong local network in the neighborhood and the city. Their main modus operandi was and still is the continuous testing of new collaborations while intervening on site. The architectural form follows the precise process of matchmaking interests, needs and potential of both new organizations, the buildings and the interiors. During all these years, this collective, factual and open approach proved to be a successful recipe to gradually develop Gundeldinger Feld into the socio-cultural hotspot it is today.

Slow transformation

Along with the assumption that design has its finality primarily in creating the conditions for others to engage, comes its task and obligation to create the conditions for slow and open transformation. When collaborative research and design lead to the identification of certain structural mechanisms of exclusion,

65 The entrance of Gundeldinger Feld at the Dornacherstrasse in Basel. An intimate new world in the neighborhood.

the logical subsequent step of testing alternatives to that exclusion is almost inevitable.

This new endeavor often starts from the existing. By identifying specific spatial structures worth preserving, people and coalitions looking for a place and willing to invest time and energy in a common cause, new matches between use, skills, the built environment and small-scale business models can be made. By iteratively connecting suitable new users with old buildings, convincing pension funds to support with long-term investments and by establishing cooperative structures to build and develop over time, a new rhythm can be found that is based on the constant quest for a temporary optimum instead of the external pressure for marginal gains.

Current times

The projects of Gundeldinger Feld and 'We kopen samen den Oudaan' should be situated in a larger attempt to challenge the reckless consumption of our planet. The forces shaping urbanity today (segregation, real estate speculation, de-industrialization, de-carbonization, digitization, etc.) redefine current categories and require transdisciplinary answers. One could say that the time has come for architecture and urban design to play out its strengths: the logics of transformation need design, dialogue and creativity to find new and integrated answers in response to a failing mode of standardization and efficiency. In situations that require redefinition, design intelligence plays a fundamental role in in finding questions and defining potential. Putting the built environment and a more sustainable quality of life to the fore both nuances and empowers architecture. From the perspective of design in dialogue, it helps to see architecture as urban design and to see urban design as urban transformation.

66 A fitness and yoga studio at Gundeldinger Feld. Finding the right match between existing buildings and the spatial requirements of the new users defined the architecture of the site.

Design in dialogue is not restricted to the inclusion of new voices (as described under knowledge of the many)—or the introduction of moments of shared interpretation (as described under safe ground for learning). Its notion of mediating challenges how architectural processes are commonly described, how project briefs are interpreted and what type of output can be expected. Finding freedom to question and introduce topics as collective ownership or adaptive re-use generates a rather unstable context. Given their alterity, previously known conditions, expectations, relations with existing institutes or power differences start changing and being interpreted in multiple ways.

These highly frictional and undefined contexts require a certain flexibility in responding. As a series of alliances with others concerned, transdisciplinary practice in architecture can be activated to address changing contexts. The forming of such new configurations can constantly challenge and test new approaches and alternative mechanisms for urban transformation.

This idea of constant reconfiguration implies that the architect or planner changes his or her own role, moving away from keeping control, towards the position of the senior improviser. This means to reorientate him- or herself towards a pragmatic practice that is constantly reorganized based on the reading of the current situation. It leads to ever changing coalitions of actors that work on a specific intervention, with a specific form that makes the most sense at that moment, at that place and with that group of people.

The focus is not on the traditional succession of research, imagination and action, but on flexible responses to limitations and possibilities within spatial developments. Sometimes this can result in a design, sometimes in a method, but also in radically different things, such as in the purchase of land or buildings, in the creation of a spinoff, or in the launch of a new communication campaign to raise awareness for a certain topic among a broad audience.

Architectural and urban practice becomes the critical navigation between the strategic and selective actions of others, tracing mechanisms of exclusion while collectively constructing possibilities for transformation.

5

Senior improviser

67　The temporary occupation of the WTC helped to imagine different ways of activating a classical floor plan.

WTC

Developed during the post-war era as a business district that could compete with La Defense in Paris and similar developments, the Modernist development of the World Trade Center in the North District of Brussels (Belgium) never fulfilled its many promises. The construction of its so-called 'Manhattan plan' caused the eviction of 11,000 people, not only demolishing their neighborhood but also erasing their memories.

While the towers still reach for the sky, it is no longer possible to ignore the situation on the ground and to stay blind to the growing gap between global ambitions and local needs and desires.

Between 2017 and 2019, 51N4E moved their design studio to the North District to initiate a lively ecosystem of actors that occupied the WTC tower. They invited students to work in and around the WTC and participated in the lectures, exhibitions, symposia and workshops organized under the umbrella of 'You are Here / IABR' and the Faculty of Architecture of the KU Leuven. Their engagement with the North District and the collaboration with different private and public partners on site resulted in a continuous exploration of partnerships and actions that redescribed their architectural profession. Triggered by both the amnesia and the unrecognized diversity of the neighborhood, the temporary occupation of the WTC created the opportunity to better understand the role of the architect in moments of urban transformation and the possibility to trigger and inspire new collective endeavors.

68　Occupying a seventies office tower in an improvised way.

69–70 During their stay in the WTC, 51N4E became part of a large community of practices ranging from artists to students and other design firms that temporarily occupied the building.

71-72 The temporary occupation of the WTC was for 51N4E an ideal moment to test new office conditions for working, teaching, leisure and new eco-systems (in collaboration with Plant & Houtgoed).

73 In the beginning of 2017, 51N4E moved their offices to the partly abandoned WTC building in the Brussels North District. A bold move that would soon become a long-lasting engagement with the place and its surrounding.

74   The team of architects and engineers responsible for the transformation of the building working on site. The new environment of WTC soon became the place to rethink the future of WTC I & II.

Strategic ambiguity

Embarking on an unknown world creates a lot of uncertainties. Out of pure intuition, it might happen that the position one takes as an organization in a project is ambiguous, in order not to run the risk of being heavily criticized or being denied access to discussions and decisions due to mistrust or antagonism already at the beginning. This was not any different in the case of the Brussels North District and 51N4E's engagement with the redevelopment of the WTC. Their move to bridge worlds of activisms, architecture and real estate development together was not uncontested and needed clarity to become productive.

A design in dialogue perspective as such challenges the notion of strategic ambiguity. It is only by being radically open that you create the opportunity for others to engage and the possibility to collectively reimagine existing restrictions and counter positions. By creating clarity on what can be expected, others can take a position and by that help to demystify the complexity of spatial transformation and make it more manageable for all actors involved. A clear position becomes as such a motive for action. The motives can be as diverse as the team, but give the possibility to act tactically and yet not lose sight of the direction.

75–76   A model to test the double height space for the reconfigured WTC, made in the offices of l'AUC in Paris. Using the experience of testing new office configurations to rethink the classic floorplan of WTC I & II.

Stadsform

In the aftermath of the campaign 'We kopen samen den Oudaan' Endeavour was triggered to find an answer on how collective ownership models could be supported and strengthened in urban redevelopment projects. Inspired by the energy and freedom to tackle urgent matters collectively and in various forms, Endeavour engaged with a wide set of responses to this pressing issue.

They introduced a new start-up 'locay' —a platform for collaborative real estate development—, organized a new fund to support cooperative housing in Flanders together with CERA and the Flemish government, and created an event space 'Stadsform' to test new hybrids of alternative real estate development, place making and events around pressing urban topics.

77   Announcement of Stadsform. The new center for dialogue of Endeavour in Antwerp.

78   'Hack the city'. One of the series of conversations initiated by Endeavour at Stadsform to discuss the impact of technology on the city.

79   Stadsform is a collaboration between a real estate developer, graphical agency and Endeavour, a unique collaboration represented in the corporate but open interior design of the space.

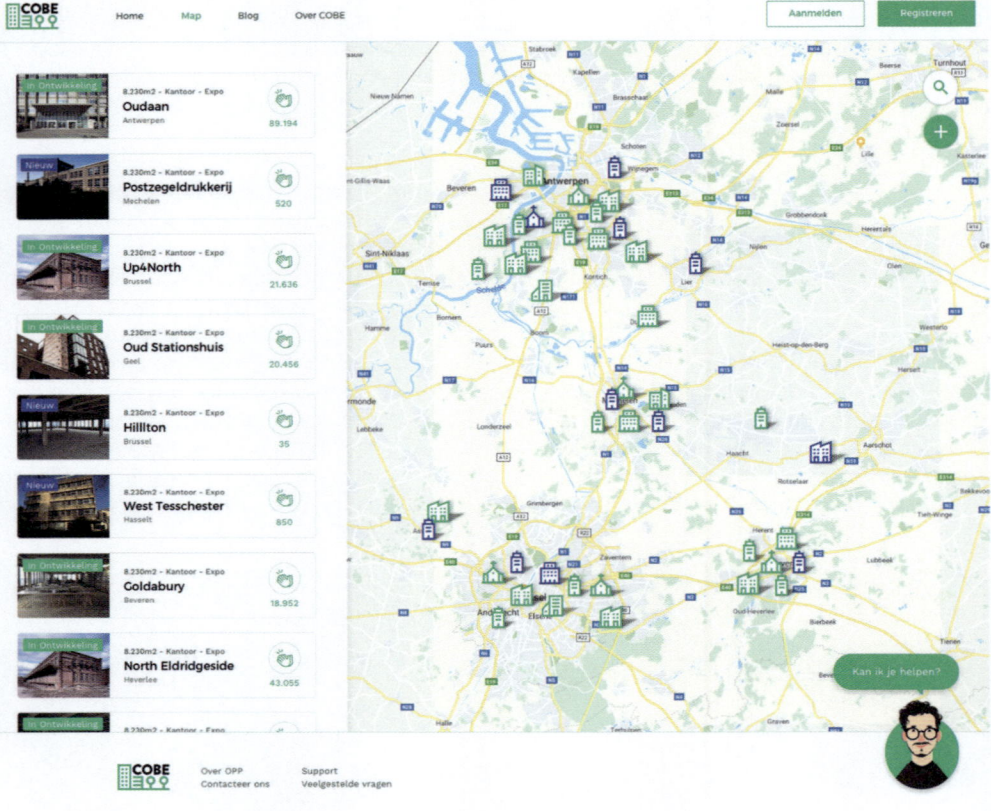

81   A first mock-up of Locay. A digital platform to support cooperative development, initiated by Endeavour after they failed to buy the Oudaan.

80   The different spaces in Stadsform are designed to host public debates, co-working spaces and neighborhood facilities.

Strategic activism

The example of Stadsform shows how design in dialogue becomes a common attitude that can continuously adapt to changing conditions and react accordingly, be it new challenges or possible collaborations. This attitude leads to a rather strategic practice that tries to continuously react to new configurations with great precision. Engaging with this increased complexity is a challenging exercise and asks for constant reflection: with whom do I work together? How can these collaborations sustain my necessary room for manoeuvre? How can this give new meaning and legitimacy to architecture and urban transformation? How can I create the opportunities to switch roles? How does this affect me and the way my practice is organized?

The strategic nature of these questions and actions recognizes the dynamic and ever-changing nature of collaboration. Instead of being limited to the continuous pressure of negotiation and consensus, strategic activism accepts the impossibility to control future actions (of others) and focuses on immediate possibilities and shared interest.

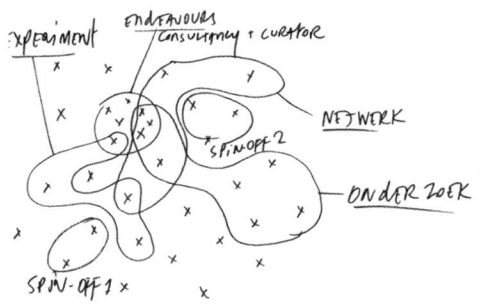

82   The organizational structure of Endeavour after the experiment of the Oudaan. Acknowledging a multiplicity of collaborative forms: from pro-active projects, developing new spin-offs to a consultancy office on social-spatial innovation.

Worker cooperative

Endeavour is registered as a worker cooperative. By organizing the work in a cooperative structure, Endeavour seeks to create the possibility for each of its collaborators to become engaged in transformative planning projects in a socially and economically sustainable way. Endeavour tries to limit the external and market-driven pressure of consultancy-based activities by developing different principles for internal solidarity.
1.   No accumulation of value: by limiting the possibilities of value accumulation, Endeavour made sure that it could always organize the company in a flexible way, supporting the direct needs of the current shareholders instead of the accumulated demands of the creditors of the past.
2.   No time registration: by excluding the economical logics of project-based work Endeavour focuses on finding a good work life balance on an organizational level. At the beginning of each year the engagement of each of the shareholders of Endeavour is defined.
3.   Investing in research and a pro-active project: each year around 30% of Endeavour's time is spent on non-funded projects or personal research trajectories.
4.   Becoming a partner: after three years and a positive evaluation everyone working at Endeavour has the possibility to become a shareholder of the company without extra costs.

Design in dialogue ultimately results in a reinterpretation of the way architectural offices are traditionally organized. Working in transformation urges practitioners and collectives to deal with complex contradictions. How do you create clarity about your own professional position and preserve enough freedom and possibilities for others to engage? How can one be completely transparent and strategic at the same time?

These questions lead to a demanding modus operandi for any organization. They require the flexibility to adapt to a wide range of circumstances and customize structures and processes ad hoc. The organization should be versatile enough to take different roles and positions as a vantage point for a project. Yet, at the same time, it needs to be stable and strong enough to administer a diverse set of responsibilities.

Both within projects and in terms of the organization of an architectural office, design in dialogue triggers the necessity to develop a structure where hierarchical supervision is neither desirable nor hoped for. Once the need for control is acknowledged as an outdated concept, people start creating stimulating and interesting working environments for themselves. They stop doing their job and start serving a role. Within these constellations the engagement is ultimately defined by the ability to share responsibility and create the conditions for others to step to the fore. These organic constellations cultivate a culture where everyone can rise to the occasion. That gives the organization the flexibility, versatility and resilience it so desperately needs to meet the demanding needs of creating and facilitating a true dialogue in our fast-paced world.

Design in dialogue fosters connections. Every instrument people develop, every milestone that is reached and every result that is achieved is a shared experience, an exchange of knowledge. Design in dialogue is a continuous, never-ending quest that reaches far beyond the scope of the architectural projects at hand. It provides the framework for a lasting, long-term paradigm shift, where every conversation, meeting, workshop, or encounter can be seen as an act of design that entails valuable contributions for the projects of architects and planners to come.

6

A culture of cooperation

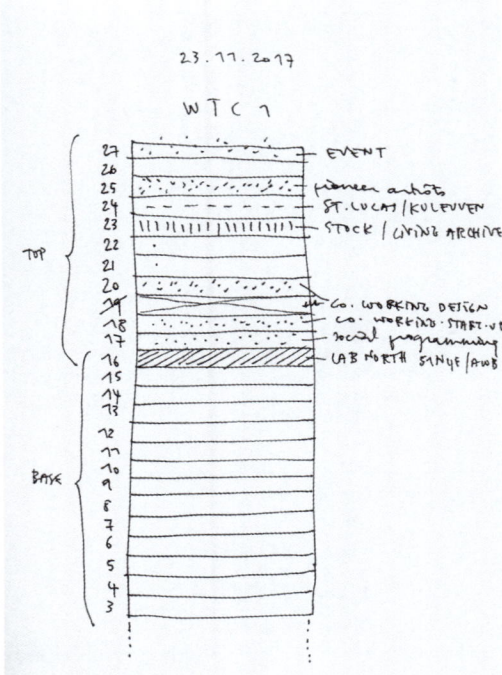

83   A test to develop a new kind of rooftop garden and a perfect place to invite the daily commuters to the neighborhood.

84   An overview of the temporary occupation of WTC 1: pioneering artist, an architectural school, social space, the office.

ZIN

The project 'ZIN in No(o)rd' aims to reuse the emblematic WTC 1 and 2 towers located in the heart of the Northern Quarter in Brussels. Instead of a simple restoration of the existing building, it is a question of adding an unprecedented dimension to the project by connecting the towers with a new volume of fourteen double-height floors. This creates a new condition for the development of a hybrid building, mixing a new way of working with housing, a hotel, sports and leisure spaces, shops and lots of vegetation.

The project is organized as an unprecedented collaboration between Befimmo and Jaspers-Eyers architects (established key players in the real estate market of Brussels and the North District in particular), 51N4E and l'AUC (which had already singled out the potential of the North District in previous studies like Brussels 2040) and Drees&Sommer and Rotor (focusing on the 'urban mining' of building materials in the current demolition and redevelopment of the WTC complex). Their first-time collaboration and the challenging condition to rethink and redefine office retail in Brussels equally challenged the partners to create a culture of experimentation and exchange that allows for a process of incremental learning.

86–87 Daily life at WTC I

85   Designing and discussing the new ZIN tower.

88   The temporary kitchen at WTC I. An important place for all users of the building to meet and exchange.

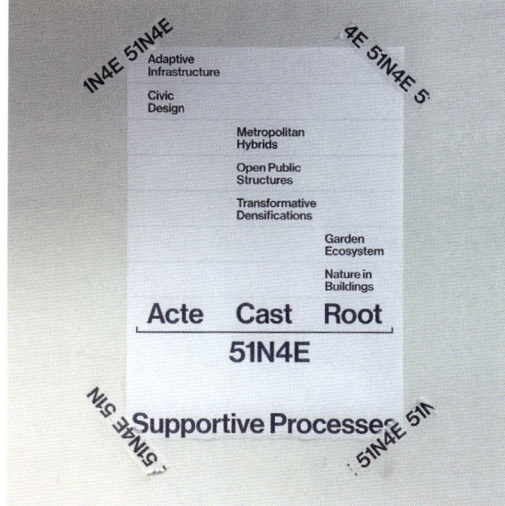

89   A first draft of the new organizational structure of 51N4E presenting different horizontal programs and smaller clusters of self-managed offices.

90   Collecting different materials of WTC. 62% of the building complex will be re-used in ZIN or other projects.

Ethics of care

Design in dialogue starts with a shared ethics of care. It is a radically inclusive approach of continuous and careful reflection on who is involved and who benefits from the proposed actions and interventions.

This ambition also applies to the development of the organizations involved, towards critical and reflexive actors. It allows to pay attention to the 'voices from the borderlands' and issues of gender and cultural diversity that are easily overlooked.

91   At the end of 2018, 51N4E moved out the WTC I tower that was soon to be transformed. One year later they moved back into the Brussels North District at CCN.

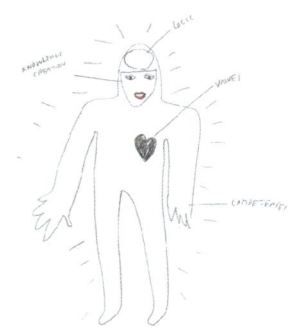

92   A drawing of 51N4E's knowledge creation agent.

93   A render of ZIN. A new hybrid typology for the Brussels North Disctrict, combining offices, housing, hotel and public amenities.

Organizational transformation

51N4E is a self-steering collective that wants to empower people to be both autonomous and connected. It does so by organizing the transversal supportive processes needed for a collaborative design culture. This collaboration platform combines the internal studios with a growing network of external partners. As such, it mirrors today's complex reality and produces an ecosystem of knowledge.

According to 51N4E, conflict can drive new and unexpected proposals. In projects, the office responds both to the specificity of situations and to patterns and questions that are shared beyond. This process thinking is organized in programs, where multiple projects regroup to feed each other with everything that is needed to turn ideas into concrete action.

The collective experience in the North District convinced the office to shuffle its organizational structure around three different studios (Acte, Cast and Root), clear in their scope and complimentary in their offer. Each of them develops its own programs and research lines in a horizontal and flexible way, while working together to address the complexity of projects.

The nomadic office

Following projects and urgencies of transformation, immediately impacts the work environment of an office. Experimenting with new settings for collaboration and finding the right scenography to rethink the output of your work is an integral part of design in dialogue. For 51N4E this transformation was triggered by the 'nomadic' office they organized during the last years. Following new phases of redevelopment in the Brussels North District, the office went through different iterations of changing the configuration of workspaces and challenged the hybrid relation between the office as a singular universe, the building as a host and the surrounding neighbourhood as a wider landscape. For 51N4E, the intensive exploration of hybrid spaces between learning, teaching

94   51N4E created a new place for exchange and dialogue on the 1,5 floors of the CCN building to experiment with new forms of open-public structures.

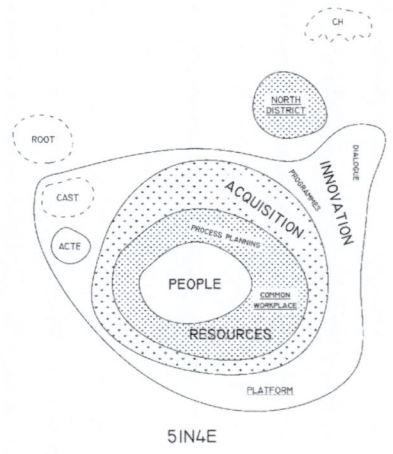

5IN4E

95   The network and work environment of 51N4E. Looking for new ways to create broader platforms of collaboration.

and producing architecture became a new mode to engage with a place. It allowed them to experiment with 'project ateliers' where large project teams intensely work together across scales, disciplines and urgencies. These new settings speak as much about the urban transformation we are designing for, as they do about the design of our own practice as part of that transformation.

96   A student atelier review on site, together with Brussels Bouwmeester Kristiaan Borret.

97   Transforming a neighborhood requires working on different scales at the same time. In the summer of 2020, 51N4E in collaboration with Plant & Houtgoed started to experiment with a temporary forest to create new ecologies and introduce shade and biodiversity in the city.

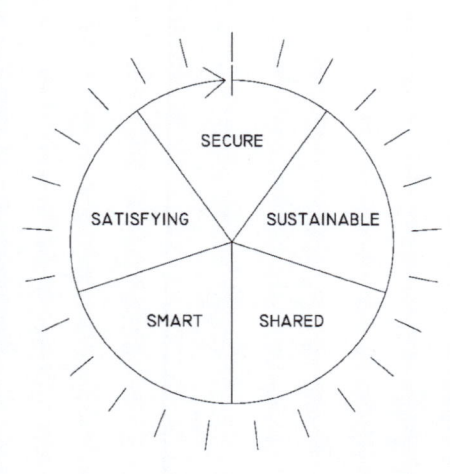

98   An overview of the goals and values 51N4E wants to integrate in their work.

De·sign in Dia·logue *(di'zain in 'daiǝlog)*
To see design as a process of dynamic learning, focusing both on the output and on ways to work together, in an attempt to exceed the expectations of everyone involved.

Outline of the idea to 'Design in Dialogue', according to the NEWROPE Chair
of Architecture and Urban Transformation

The NEWROPE Chair of Architecture and Urban Transformation explores and promotes the idea to design in dialogue. This idea is based on the belief that design benefits from the input of a multitude of perspectives. As part of this exploration, the NEWROPE Chair developed the Design in Dialogue Lab at the ONA building in Zürich-Oerlikon, which offers a variety of configurations that allow to come together, to test new ideas and practices. Combining theatrical elements with DiD tools for co-production, the lab offers the conditions to reflect, share and relax in a variety of work sessions, informal gatherings and public events.

ADAPTING TO AN EXHAUSTED WORLD

Why do we keep on talking about architecture as *the art of construction?* Being an architect and designing buildings myself, I know the joy of creating them, and it is easy to love that work when you are close to it. But when zooming out, and no longer looking at buildings but seeing the built environment, it becomes harder to appreciate the quality of so many buildings, constructions and infrastructure. I often ask myself the question: Wouldn't it be better if architects start dreaming about building less rather than about building more? To focus on existing built environment instead?

Starting to work at ETH[1] is for me a way to investigate these questions. The first act when I got appointed was to rename the chair from Architecture and Urban Design to Architecture and Urban Transformation, orienting the focus away from the connotation the German word *Städtebau*[2] has of building new and ever more cities. This renaming isn't done to polarize. It is more to be alert about what we need to avoid–to consume space in a careless way–and also to acknowledge the precarious situation we are in and how architecture is often instrumentalized in a consumerist approach to space and material.

Acknowledging something starts by describing it, and upon entering the ETH I came across such a description of the changing built environment compiled in a book as massive as the condition it looks at. *Mirroring Effects*–co-written by Marc Angélil and Carey Siress–takes on the challenge of describing the urbanized environment as a phenomenon that spans across the world. It compiles a series of case studies that "unfold as real-life tales chronicling mutually reinforcing processes that bind urbanization to integrated world capitalism." The description is as thick as the book, heavy also from the despair that comes with looking so closely at the world around us. But in the last chapter, something else is happening. This chapter feels different from the others. Rather than an ending, this piece of text is an envoi. *Environment-making,*[3] it states.

ENVIRONMENT-MAKING

Amidst all the jargon that is required to flesh out observations and contradictions of contemporary urban territories, the heading of this chapter stands out in all its simplicity. It urges us to refocus the agenda for architecture and urban design, understanding it as a practice that should acknowledge that we are inhabiting Earth's *critical zone,* a thin layer[4] with a changing climate that is much more fragile than we think. It invites us to look at this condition with care, attention and detail despite the fact that to start taking this perspective is in itself overwhelming and even destabilizing.

Invitation accepted? The call to reorient architecture from making buildings to making environments may be brushed aside as too ambitious, as trying to confront problems that are too big to handle. Or it can be ridiculed as being too naive, even if this naiveté is a rational response to a crisis that is the result of the way humans deal with their environment. We are depleting the environment as if we are not part of it, blind to how our exploitative relationship to our own habitat will have disruptive consequences.

To make environment is an attempt to change the extractive nature of cities, by detecting, strengthening and building other value systems, with smaller and more grounded or localized feedback loops. It comes from a desire to shift towards a more nurturing or healing approach to the places we live in and to care for environments and everything that depends on them, in ways we still have to learn and discover. Even if we do not know enough about climate change and all that comes with it, there is one thing that we know for sure: we will have to learn how to adapt and shift from our current practices to new and other practices.

As part of 51N4E, a Brussels-based practice that concerns itself with matters of space, I have been confronted with the uphill battle that this entails. A project like Skanderbeg Square in the Albanian capital Tirana was a huge effort, requiring time and patience to transform the center of a car-dominated city into a car-free place that reveals a whole different set of values and possible behaviors. A square does not seem much at first sight. In terms of surface it feels like a fragile speckle when looked at from the perspective of the *thin layer*.

But it has been empowering to witness–once the redesign became a tangible reality–what a square can trigger in terms of new experiences. It has become a concrete reference point and a symbol within and beyond the context of the city, by valuing its own past and by offering a green belt that installs a new ecosystem in what used to be a barren traffic junction. Suddenly, being a pedestrian or riding a bike had something noble to it. Also the way the municipality took the adaptation of the square, and the possibilities it brought as a catalytic moment to start changing the traffic from the center outwards, has had tremendous effects. It somehow makes you reconcile with your own naiveté and realize the power of focusing on environment-making.

LOOKING WITH CARE

Skanderbeg Square stands as an example that this discovery will not just be about looking forward, but also about looking back. For ages, and especially before industrialization started, due to the simple means and natural materials architecture has often been a human activity almost organically creating a harmonious relationship with its environment. It is important to realize that the problems we need to face are not just about finding new and technological solutions. It is equally important to look with care, at what is there and how it could gain new meaning. To try and understand the interdependencies and how they could shift by bringing in new elements or taking some away.

To a certain extent, this approach is unspectacular and inspired by a certain humility. This does not mean to shy away from ambition but to let these ambitions be infused by the constraints of what is there and by adapting to them. In sync with how the effects of climate change will require all of us to incrementally adapt, architecture and design could refrain from starting from scratch and instead work from what is already there in all its complexity. It could become an art of adaptation.

To make environment, we have to learn to design for integrated and long-term value and not just for the solution to the problem that is on our table right now. It means to become aware that you are dealing with wicked problems, for which we need to develop solutions that are not right or wrong, but better or worse. To make environment requires us to become sensitive to what is already there–both tangible and intangible–and how it can be woven into a new configuration. It is about the effort of not just focusing on built matter, but also on how spaces are used or abused, lived in or worn out, and specific meanings and possibilities that are often overlooked, unseen and ignored. Architect and urbanist Paola Viganò beautifully talks about this approach as *projects that describe*. Her thesis is that "descriptive projects are those that do not deny and do not claim to change the structural attributes of contemporary space, but instead reveal the elements of rationality contained in those very characteristics."[5]

WEAVING PATTERNS

For any architect, this sensitivity means that one can no longer focus on a project as a singular object but instead that one should start mentally unravelling a project, by opening it up, making it porous and starting to see it as a series of contributions to a larger whole. The mental image we make of these contributions and how they should perform makes a difference, however. One way to look at it is to consider them as pieces of a puzzle, neatly interlocking but clearly delineated. This view is efficient, and still dominant, but also highly problematic since this type of operational organization easily produces spatial discontinuity. It tends to make sense from the perspective of the different spatial designers, but very often doesn't make sense from a user perspective.

The different design dynamics are not activated to achieve integration. With this type of organization, we more often tend to produce fragmentation.

As an alternative image to the puzzle pieces stands the image of the semi-lattice[6], as proposed by architect and mathematician Christopher Alexander. Based on his mathematical investigations of design in *Notes on the Synthesis of Form* he describes the built environment, in a subsequent book titled *A Pattern Language*, as a series of spatial and interlocking patterns. Together these patterns start to weave an environment, across scales, from the brick to the city to the metropolitan region (and today he would probably say: across the *thin layer*).

In Alexander's description of architecture, he values relationships as the essence of design. Apart from describing the interrelations between patterns, Alexander is also attentive to how patterns allow to describe the ways in which architecture enables a social construction. What is valuable in his work is that his way of looking is giving value to what is seemingly trivial.[7] The focus is not only on materials and space, but also on how these interrelate and interact and on the meaning for life they generate and trigger.

In his view of architecture as an art of adaptation, the work of the architect becomes to pack different patterns together in a sensitive and sensible way, and to design towards their integration. With the goal of environment-making in mind, Alexander's work on patterns is very meaningful to revisit. By conceptualizing the environment as the packing of patterns we can more easily imagine it as open-ended and in a constant state of transformation. The environment can always be adapted and will in some way always stay unadapted.

At the same time, there is something about Alexander's work that feels contradictory to the open-endedness we imagine when we talk about transformation. Maybe–on a more cultural level–his description of how to reach harmony feels at odds with how we live and experience our realities today. Looking at contemporary urban environments, it feels difficult and even counterproductive to desire the sense of wholeness that Alexander is referring to, especially when we zoom out beyond the scale of the building. Friction or disharmony feels like a fundamental aspect of how we perceive the world around us today and is without a doubt inherent to the crises and changes we are confronted with. To face and facilitate the much needed transitions and to create the conditions that will enable it to happen, it is fundamental to embrace these tensions. In urban areas which suffered from the compartmentalization Alexander was criticizing, the challenge is to synthesize, not to sanitize. A small experiment we conducted in the North District,[8] highlights what this entails. Over the summer, on the sidewalk and the adjoining parking bays between the large-scale boulevard with its monumental rows of trees and the three-story marble base of the

Diagram showing the shift towards environment-making

In their book *Mirroring Effects* architects Marc Angélil and Cary Siress introduce the concept of *environment-making*. This concept challenges the discipline of architecture, which normally focuses on single buildings, to get involved in shaping the environment by taking into account the interactions and co-evolutions between things, and between things and their surroundings.

Together with other disciplines (e.g. sociology, transportation systems, infrastructure and territorial planning), architecture is co-responsible for the production of the social and spatial environments that we collectively inhabit. Designing for environments requires systems thinking: thinking in relations, thinking in dynamic and interacting models and thinking with time.

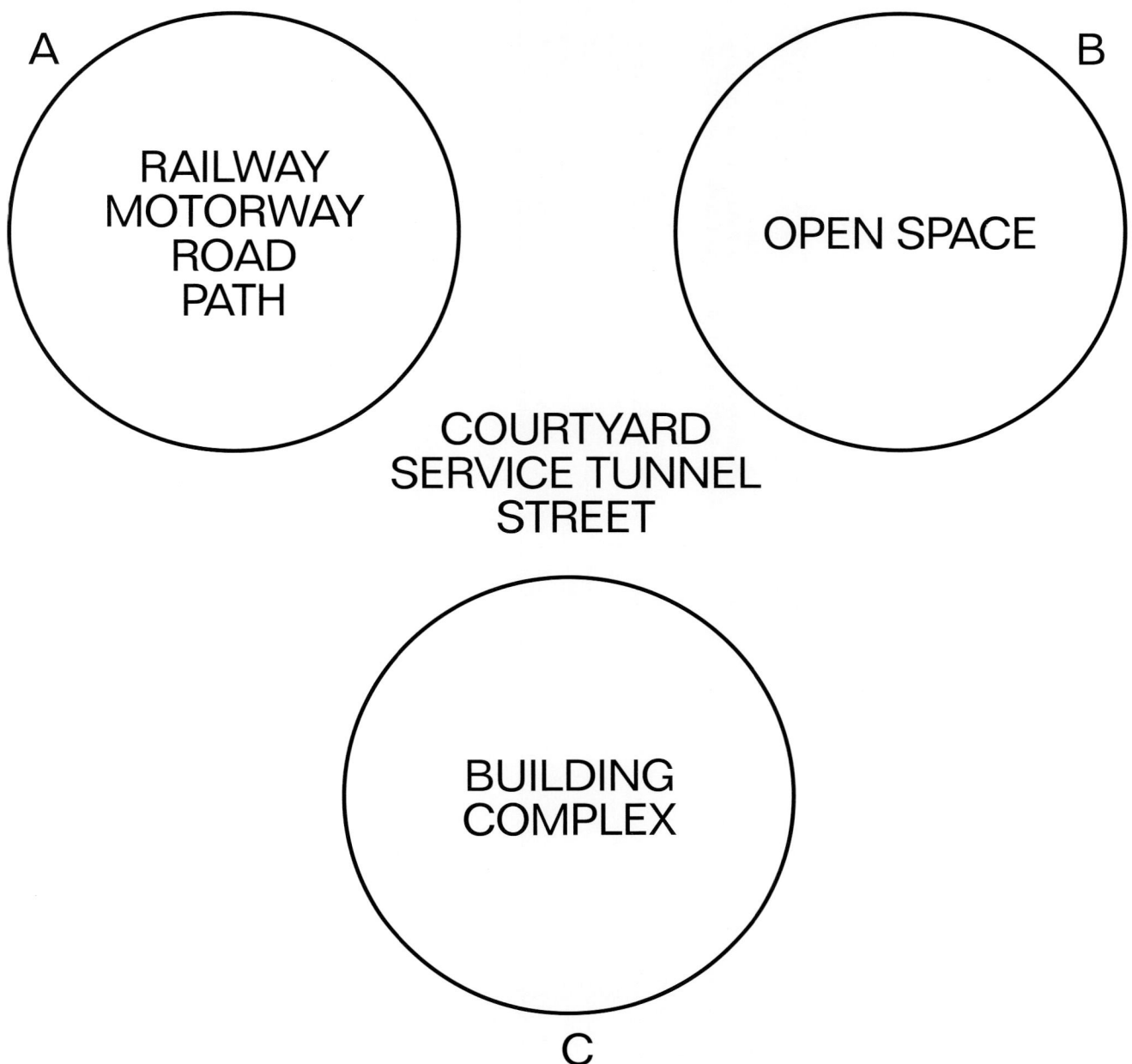

A railway
motorway
road
path

B open space

courtyard
service tunnel
street

C building
complex

A) Transport Engineer   B) Landscape Architect   C) Architect

Diagram showing how functionalist planning conceptualizes the responsibilities of:
A) the transport engineer, B) the landscape architect and C) the architect, while indicating the
spaces falling in between

Functionalist planning processes that focus on clear delineation of responsibilities and domains of expertise have trouble capturing the ambivalent values of the spaces that are shared and perform multiple purposes at once. This challenge of integration is not just a question of what things are and how they are made to perform in a diversity of ways, but also how their performance and relations are thought, managed and allowed by whoever is responsible. It is as much a spatial challenge as an organizational one, embedded in how society is or could be organized.

unfinished WTC4 tower, a small patch of (mobile) urban forest has been planted. This patch simply adds a layer to the spatial set-up of the district. Physically nothing more than an addition of furniture, plants and artificial irrigation, it weaves a new pattern into the space, enabling a whole new set of uses. This intervention is a response to the tensions found in the initial spatial set-up of the base and boulevard, and forms an example of finding new ways of how to deal with them. It is not, however, an intervention that 'repairs' the boulevard. More than anything, it disturbs the current spatial layout. It is almost like a physical reminder that things could also be different and that these two realities can co-exist and could continue to do so.

GOING THROUGH THE WEB OF THINGS

Often interventions are not as subtle and soft as the mobile forest. Excavating a hidden river or partly dismantling a tower, as will happen in the North District in Brussels, are crucial acts to reconnect parts of the environment, even if the brutality of these actions seems – at first sight – to be at odds with the nurturing effect they aim to have. In the process of design, adapting something is not just about trying to restore something or making it whole. In my view, it is sufficient to see these interventions as active agents that change the game, destabilize or rewire a situation, to give it new meaning and to create new relationships and values. The challenge here is not to try and capture everything, but rather to question what could be the most minimal intervention with the maximum effect. Design is not seen as a final solution, but as a transformative process which is intervention-driven, with strategic steps towards another reality, steps which are all temporary in their own way.

Sometimes an action can be as simple as changing a behavioral condition. I remember very vividly the way the fountain in the central roundabout of the North District has been made accessible for only one day. The only physical action it required was to reroute the traffic for that single day, and suddenly the performance of the space shifted as if from night to day. What Pool is Cool – the designers of that intervention – demonstrated with their action, is that it all starts by carefully looking and assessing the potential of a given situation. It also showed – to their own despair – how difficult it often is to change habits, because they have ramifications on many different levels. In order to make that type of adaptation, they had to unravel all the inherent connections and liabilities attached to that roundabout and understand how it is embedded in how society operates. Designing entailed activities like collecting a sample of the water and doing laboratory tests or arranging municipal police clearances (from two municipalities, in fact). To see the work of

adaptation as inherently multi-layered and conflictual makes it much easier to imagine how it could work in a contemporary context. Design actions can be seen as interventions with a catalytic effect, creating leverage and impact.[9] This requires navigating back and forth between action and reflection in a continuous learning process. Design should in that respect not only be understood as aiming for a physical result. In the case of the temporary pool, the long term impact is to make people see a space in a new light and anchor a new experience in the collective imagination.

When it comes to solutions, there is no single truth, only an array of possibilities, as moments in an ongoing process of transformation. Seeing design as intervention-driven means that the context is not considered as a complex whole that can be mastered or controlled, but is about looking for ways to engage with reality in all its complexity, by caring for the consequences of your actions and by actively learning from them. As an example: when working in the military submarine base in Saint Nazaire[10] in France, there was no way of changing the context we worked in. The sheer mass of the submarine base is simply too big to substantially alter. What we could do is to look for new meaning while accepting the identity and values people ascribe to it.

In this respect, the conceptual frameworks developed in the realm of heritage preservation and adaptive reuse are also very relevant to consider in the context of more general urban transformation processes. While being sensitive to both material and immaterial values, opportunities for adaptive reuse within the built environment can be approached through the concept of *packages of sense*, or the idea that places consist of many layers of meaning that were built up over time and can be either accepted, transformed or suppressed by design actions.

RADICAL OPENNESS

Working with *packages* or *patterns*, woven into the things around us, we start to confront complexity by not just looking at the whole but by trying to discern the structural form and relationships between the various layers. This is not so much a design methodology, but rather a design attitude or even a design sensibility. In an uncanny combination of ambition and humility, it is about working towards integrated values, beyond the scope of the design contribution and in anticipation of the ramifications that are being triggered. In respect to this design sensibility, Alexander writes about the designer's use of patterns in almost mystical terms: "But once a person can relax, and let the forces in the situation act through him as if he were a medium, then he sees that the language, with very little help, is able to do almost all the work, and that the building shapes itself.

This is the importance of the void. A person who is free, and egoless, starts with a void, and lets the language generate the necessary forms out of this void. He overcomes the need to hold onto an image, the need to control the design and he is comfortable with the void and confident that the laws of nature, formulated as patterns, acting in his mind, will together create all that is required."[11] In this quote, he describes design as the process in which there is a fluidity between action and reflection and both start to inform each other, on the condition that a designer is capable of waiting for the meaning to emerge before taking the next step. Alexander's quote recalls descriptions of martial arts practitioners, who are able to respond to unexpected changes in their environment and seems to echo the idea of the designer as a reflective practitioner as described by philosopher and professor in urban planning, Donald Schön.[12]

Even if Alexander's description has romantic overtones, the idea that design is often about waiting for the meaning to emerge is a condition that I clearly recognize. I remember landscape architect Dirk Sijmons of H+N+S, who was talking about our collaborative project for Istanbul in terms of judo, alluding to being in a state of receptivity.[13] And although this notion of the designer is in itself beautiful, there is a very important aspect of the practice that neither Schön nor Alexander explicitly mentions – apart from the exclusively male description of the designer – namely the collective nature of the entire design and transformation process.

Both seem to have little to say about how design acquires meaning in relation to others or other practices. In dealing with the challenges of environment-making, where so many voices have a stake, design is also about becoming aware of externalities and of the links and connections that are often disregarded. It is a challenge that can only be taken up if design is considered as a collective endeavor, in dialogue with others. It is about the positions you take as a designer, which is in part about the ability to collaborate. And beyond that, about the ability to deal with different perspectives on reality and the ways in which a design reinforces or ignores parts of the lived realities of people. And to make it even more uncomfortable: it is also about dealing with the value others attach to your own practice.

It is when we start considering all of these aspects that we start to talk about design in dialogue. The ambition to radically open up to others and to design in dialogue means that designers have to expand the notion of patterns. This integral perspective starts when we not only look at patterns of space, but also start to include social and cultural patterns of practice, of dialogue, of collective problem-finding.[14] It means that patterns are not just described in general terms, but also in the multiple ways in which they are perceived differently by the various actors involved in the process.

THOUGHT PATTERNS

In order to understand how different people look at and try to understand a situation from a wide range of perspectives, the work of social scientist and psychologist, Otto Laske can serve as a powerful tool.[15] His Dialectical Thought Form (DTF) framework highlights different ways how to think and clarifies the wide variety of thought forms from a perspective of human cognitive development. He not only includes context thinking–the main focus architects tend to take into consideration–but also adds process, relation and transformation thinking to the equation.

With the framework, Otto Laske describes in depth 28 dialectical thought forms. These forms are best understood as devices helpful in probing the four moments of dialectic from different perspectives in many different situations where communication is paramount. He writes: "The ultimate goal of seeking to understand the underlying structure of movement-in-thought is to increase one's own and others' ability to anticipate, connect, and solve issues at a deeper level. The profound idea behind the framework is the awareness of the immense flexibility of the mind in seeing things in a new way, different from established cultural, social, and organizational conventions and ideologies."[16] Considering environment-making through the lens of the DTF Framework, the focus shifts from architecture as a built result to architecture as a process of transformation.

Using the framework as an internal reflection tool in the project of Skanderbeg Square and its long and tumultuous process, empowered 51N4E to shift and broaden the perspective on our own design along the way.[17] By trying to understand the different perspectives of the numerous stakeholders, and by trying to adjust to what developmental steps we thought we might be able to trigger, our understanding of the transformative capacity of the process gradually evolved. What started as the setting of an architectural frame, gradually morphed into a process where the design was reconsidered as a series of subprojects, each with their own goals and alliances. What the DTF Framework elicited – even if we didn't fully grasp it–was an acceptance of the different speeds of development and degrees of quality these different subprojects could have, also based on the degrees of complexity of perspectives of the stakeholders involved. Eventually, when we started to see the green belt that surrounded the square in our design not just as a park but as the beginning–or as a prototype–of a new ecology for the whole city, we managed to effectively broaden also our own perspective from a contextual to a transformational one. This is one of the experiences that revealed to me the potential for designers to broaden the purely contextual-thinking with process-thinking, relationship-thinking, and transformation-thinking. Process-thinking is about becoming

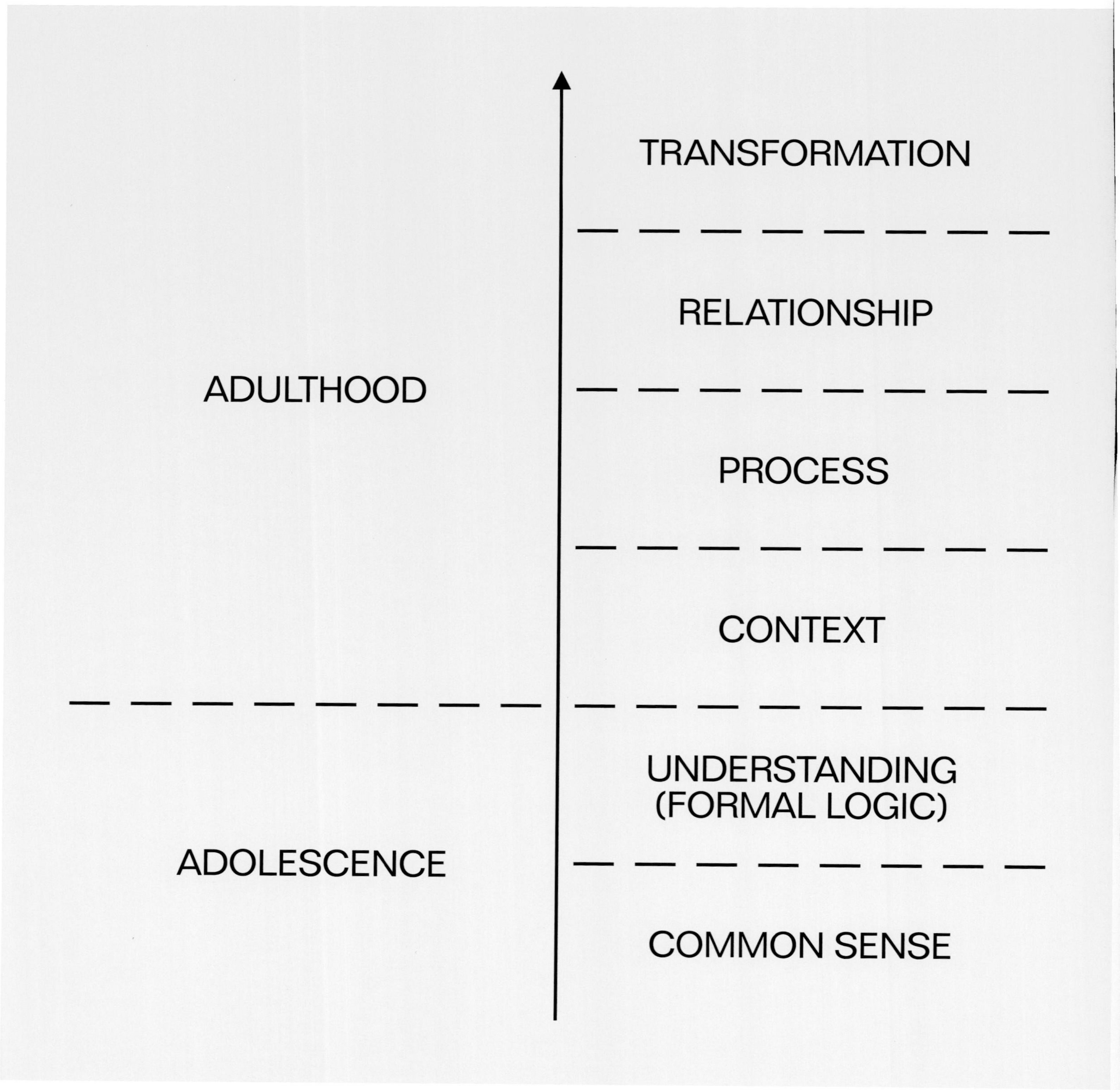

TRANSFORMATION

- - - - - - - - - -

RELATIONSHIP

ADULTHOOD - - - - - - - - - -

PROCESS

- - - - - - - - - -

CONTEXT

- - - - - - - - - - - - - - - - - - -

UNDERSTANDING
(FORMAL LOGIC)

ADOLESCENCE - - - - - - - - -

COMMON SENSE

*Redrawn diagram based on the work of Otto Laske demonstrating four developmental steps
from logical to dialectical thinking*

*Source: Laske, Otto. "A New Approach to Dialog: Teaching the Dialectical Thought Form
Framework – Part I: Foundations of Real-World Dialog."* Integral Leadership Review,
April/June 2017.

The Dialectical Thought Form (DTF) Framework was developed by Otto Laske, a multidisciplinary consultant, coach, teacher and scholar in the social sciences. The DTF Framework is a model that empowers individuals and groups of people to critically listen to, and question, each others' thinking about the world in terms of the structure (and not only the content) of their thinking. It is based on the assumption that human consciousness progresses through different phases of cognitive development, as shown above: from acknowledging multiple contexts and frames of reference (Context) to understanding the difference between past, present and future and experience change over time (Process) to recognizing patterns of interaction and influence (Relationship) and, ultimately, seeing the developmental potential of situations (Transformation).

DTF was conceived as a dialectic social practice and can serve as a way to discover one's own movements-in-thought in exchange with others. In any process of transformation, it helps one to think more clearly about oneself and relationships with others on a behavioral level (how am I doing in the group?), a social-emotional level (what should I do and for whom?) and a cognitive level (what can I do and what are my options).

A	YELLOW
B	BLUE
C	RED
D	GREEN
E	WHITE

A) Power & Politics   B) Rational Process   C) Seduce People
D) Action Learning   E) Dynamic Learning

Redrawn diagram based on the work of Léon de Caluwé and Hans Vermaak demonstrating an overview of five change paradigms

Source: Learning to Change: A Guide for Organization Change Agents, *Léon de Caluwé and Hans Vermaak, SAGE Publications, 2003.*

In *Change Paradigms: An Overview* social researchers and management consultants Léon de Caluwé and Hans Vermaak present five fundamentally different ways of thinking about transformation, each representing different belief systems and convictions about how change works, the kind of interventions that are effective, how to change people, etc. They are labeled by color: yellow, blue, red, green and white print thinking. Each is based upon a family of theories about change. For example, in blue-print thinking it is assumed that people or things will only change if a clearly specified plan or result is defined and executed. On the other hand, white-print thinking uses self-organization and dynamic learning to navigate complex and unpredictable situations.

These five models function as communication and diagnostic tools and provide a map of possible change strategies. The change paradigms provide a common language between those involved in processes of transformation to characterize dominant paradigms and blind spots in groups or organizations. And it offers so-called 'change agents' a tool for reflection: What are your own assumptions? What is your key competence for bringing about change? What are your limitations? And (how) can you change yourself?

aware of the dynamics of emerging change and the patterns of interaction and embeddedness of processes. Relationship-thinking is about the limits of separation and structural and implicit relationships between actors and their actions. Transformation-thinking is about sensing limits of stability or friction, valuing developmental potential and understanding how identity remains itself under constant transformation.

DESIGN IN DIALOGUE

Looking at all of these dimensions, the array of perspectives at one's disposal increases enormously, together with the ways to conceptualize and activate design. It can be about rethinking the material configuration, but also about what emerges when steps of an intervention are taken. Or how a design process establishes new relationships and even how a situation can shift from one state into another in a deeply transformative way. Looking from these multiple perspectives is crucial when working towards environment-making. Unpacking the built environment using both the spatial patterns of Alexander and the thought patterns of Laske (or the thought forms, as he calls them) allows to include a focus on more immaterial things. It helps to turn the practice of urban transformation into a more process-oriented discipline that actively builds on the social sciences to construct a design, proactively becoming sensitive to the meanings that emerge along the way.

Based on this expanded notion of patterns, when we scale up beyond the building and look at the environment, architecture can start to be considered as a practice that not only relates to and integrates the work of several technical and engineering disciplines, but also operates as a social practice that consciously works together with other humanist practices: community facilitators, organizational coaches, artists and cultural workers, historians and ethnographers, social and political scientists. The knowledge in these fields can help to reach beyond the boundaries of architectural offices and academia. In comparison to the processes of system thinking inherent to the engineering disciplines, the integration of the humanist disciplines can activate the necessary complimentary movement: to achieve a closer proximity to situations and be more connected to the senses and to life. This only holds true, however, if the humanist practices are willing and able to operate in an open dialogue with the design profession and others. It has to be clear that this is very often not the case. Also in these fields there is often the challenge to go beyond problem-solving and quantitative approaches. The shift towards more openness will be necessary to create possibilities rather than to close them. Once more, the redesign of Skanderbeg Square serves as a great illustration.

At a certain moment in the process we decided to count the traffic, especially pedestrian flows. Rather than setting it up as a purely quantitative exercise, it was considered as a qualitative one,[18] opening up to multiple dimensions, by also probing for perceptions, desires and even dreams about what the square could be. Even if the general framework of the design was already defined, this operation revealed in a lot of different ways how details could be altered, improved and executed to allow for many of these insights and needs to be reflected and accommodated. Rather than in the purely statistical data that was collected and the question whether it validated design choices or not, the value came from the dialogue that was triggered. By expanding the question of counting, multiple perspectives were revealed and could be considered. The data offered snapshots into a multi-layered reality, as another fertile ground to inform and deepen the design work once more. Even if it was just a patchwork[19] of insights and observations, and no claim could be made of it being representative of all the possible perspectives, the generated input was still much richer than if the design would have been purely based on assumptions and on the observation of a single designer.

This example reveals a crucial tension in how dialogue can be interpreted, differing between the problem-solving and the dialogic approach. In the first approach dialogue is goal-oriented, described as using rational and analytic processes that can be contained in a set of best practice models or toolboxes. This approach assumes that dialogue can be planned and managed. There seems to be a belief that there is a set of right behaviors and competences, and even a sense of the truth. In the second approach, dialogue creates the conditions that allow integration and even transcendence of different perspectives. It considers dialogue as an exploration through the critical interplay of different viewpoints. This meeting of minds is seen as a situation that is socially constructed and the outcome of a process of reasonable inquiry. Attention is paid to what has not been addressed yet, to the perspectives that are underrepresented, and to those things that create tensions with dominant views on reality. This approach to dialogue is essentially about the development of a fluidity of thinking[20] and the associated belief that something like an universal truth does not exist.

DECENTERING THE ARCHITECT

The first approach to dialogue immediately brings up the notion of participation and the way this notion is too often understood in planning processes and increasingly in architectural design processes. It is used not so much to talk about empowerment and designing together, but to talk about ways to validate decisions that are already made, or to define some margins for negotiation, in order to arrive at a situation where a few minor concerns can be negotiated and absorbed. To put it even in a more harsh way: dialogue is often used as a way to validate power, rather than to question or share it. This interpretation of participation has made many designers very suspicious of dialogue. Unfortunately, this defensive reaction makes many of us miss out on the opportunity to open up to the second possibility, which is a whole different world of practice.

To be clear: we are not talking about a small difference here. Where the notion of participation can be understood as adding a small component to a process of blueprint planning–almost like an afterthought–the notion of design in dialogue signals a new beginning. It is about the promise–and the challenge–to radically open up to others and share design and decision-making processes in ways that fundamentally change the game. When we say design in dialogue, we talk–and dream–about this other emergent practice, and other ways of including multiple perspectives and ways of constructing reality.

This expanded notion of design in dialogue implies a natural and crucial shift towards a discipline that can only perform in a transdisciplinary or even postdisciplinary way. With designers not just defined by their own discipline, but by the fluidity with which their practices move between the fields of design and adjacent domains–including the arts, politics, economy, anthropology and ecology–and beyond these disciplines, by involving civil society and non-professionals. But is an architect or urban designer in a position to do this? Like many other disciplines, the architectural profession is often confined to its respective domains of knowledge and expertise, without the power or shared language to go beyond it.

A shift to a different constellation is necessary. Towards a practice of practices working together, transforming space and the ways we inhabit it through a series of connected actions, merging multiple perspectives. Looking from divergent points of view enables us to activate a situation in different ways, according to what is most relevant at a given moment in time. As Francesco Garutti, curator at the Canadian Center of Architecture, describes it: "The building itself, in this new ecology of practice, is now more than ever just one piece of an extended system–the final outcome of a long sequence of actions undertaken in the transformation of a territory by a web of agents. But it is also a mechanism designed to resolve–or rather, to reveal–the conflicts, anomalies, and contradictions intrinsic to a new, expanded definition of context. Decomposed, dissected, and reassembled, context–the people, tools, policies, economies, times, and scales with which the architect interacts–not only generates the conditions within which to work, but is in fact *the place itself* in which and with which to operate."21

Already now, there are experimental spatial practices that have shaped an approach where the initial focus is not on the construction of a building, for example in the work of Barbara Buser, architect and co-founder of both architectural practice baubüro in situ and Denkstatt in Basel or in the work of Natassa Dourida, engineer and founder of the community-run sociocultural center Communitism in Athens. Both share a love for buildings, manifesting itself by reactivating and taking care of existing ones and not so much by the urge to design and build new ones. These practices are intriguing reversals of the more conventional idea of what the architects' job is. They are hands-on experiments in shaping an environment through the interaction with the network of people they assemble to use and inhabit it. A similar shift of focus towards using behavior and management as design tools can be found in the realm of landscape architecture. For example, in the work of Teresa Galí-Izard the drawing is not used to create new forms, but serves as a tool to describe the complexity of the context. This context is not redrawn, but rather regenerated by imagining patterns of occupation that will gradually–over time–enhance soils and only (re-)create landscapes as the result of that process.

From a classical design point of view, these practices are destabilizing. And similar to environment-making, the openness that comes with designing from this perspective might even sound naive and appear as a weakness. While on the contrary, it is a conscious choice, and each of the three people I mentioned just now talk about it with a conviction that is anything but naive.

PRODUCING CHANGE

The goal is not to deny the fact that processes of architecture and urban transformation are more often than not set up as blueprint processes, focused on executing a pre-established plan. This is still part and parcel of the profession. The architect is generally activated in an instrumental way, required to execute a task rather than to find out where to make a difference. Dealing with complexity is often only interpreted as being able to navigate opaque political decision making and trying to make sure that participation happens in a controlled way and disturbs as little as possible.

What design in dialogue and the underlying ambition of environment-making try to establish is something else. It tries to make the shift towards a process that is based on collective learning. It tries to fully embrace the dynamic nature of any transformation process. It tries to design a process that can be fed and enhanced by multiple perspectives, where interventions also become intercrossings.22 Hans Vermaak and Léon de Caluwé, organizational development experts, differentiate between five different

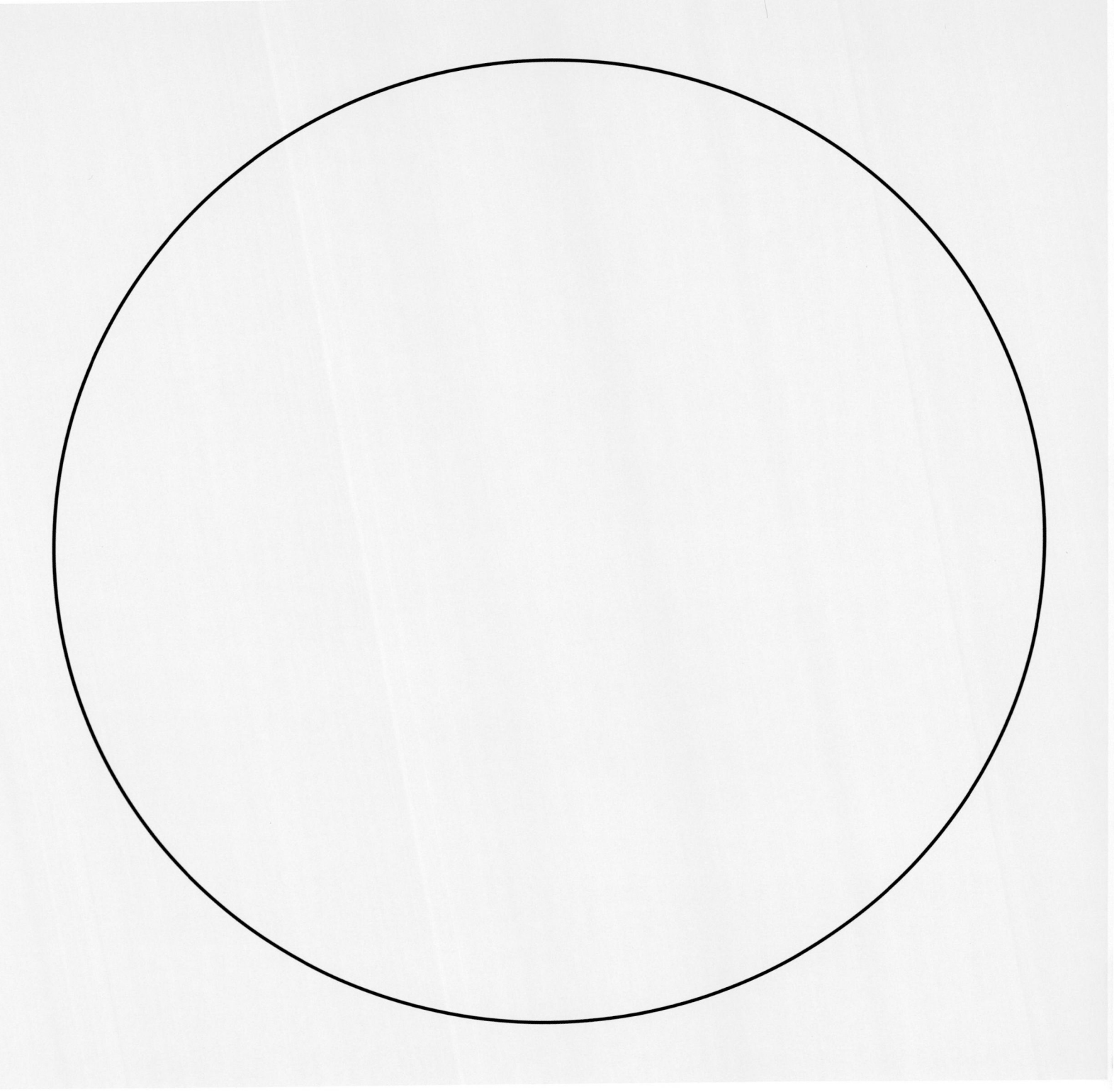

Redrawn diagram based on the work of Angelo Bucci titled 'The Human Thin Layer'

Source: SATELLIGHTS orbiting over an extremely thin layer of life [zenith and horizon], *Angelo Bucci, 2017. Published in The World as an Architectural Project, Hashim Sarkis, Roi Salgueiro Barrio & Gabriel Kozlowski (eds.), MIT Press, 2020*

This circle depicts the Earth's boundary as a thin layer of approximately 3,5 kilometers that constitutes the inhabitable realm of the planet. What appears as a single line, actually consists of two parallel lines when zooming in: the inner and outer circles of the thin layer. Angelo Bucci based this bandwidth on the range of altitudes of capital cities around the world: La Paz, in Bolivia, is the highest capital city in the world, situated at more than 3,500 meters above sea level in the Andes. Baku, in Azerbaijan, is the world's lowest lying capital city at 28 meters below sea level. Virtually all urban life on our planet occurs between these two extremes.

At an architectural scale, 3,5 kilometers seems incredibly thick. However, when seen at the scale of the world, it is almost negligible. In this thin, porous and permeable layer, which French philosopher Bruno Latour calls the *Critical Zone,* human life is not a passive act or adapting to an inert environment; it transforms that environment. If we want to sustain (human) life, we have to accept that humans cannot escape the 'thin layer' and design the conditions for cohabitation.

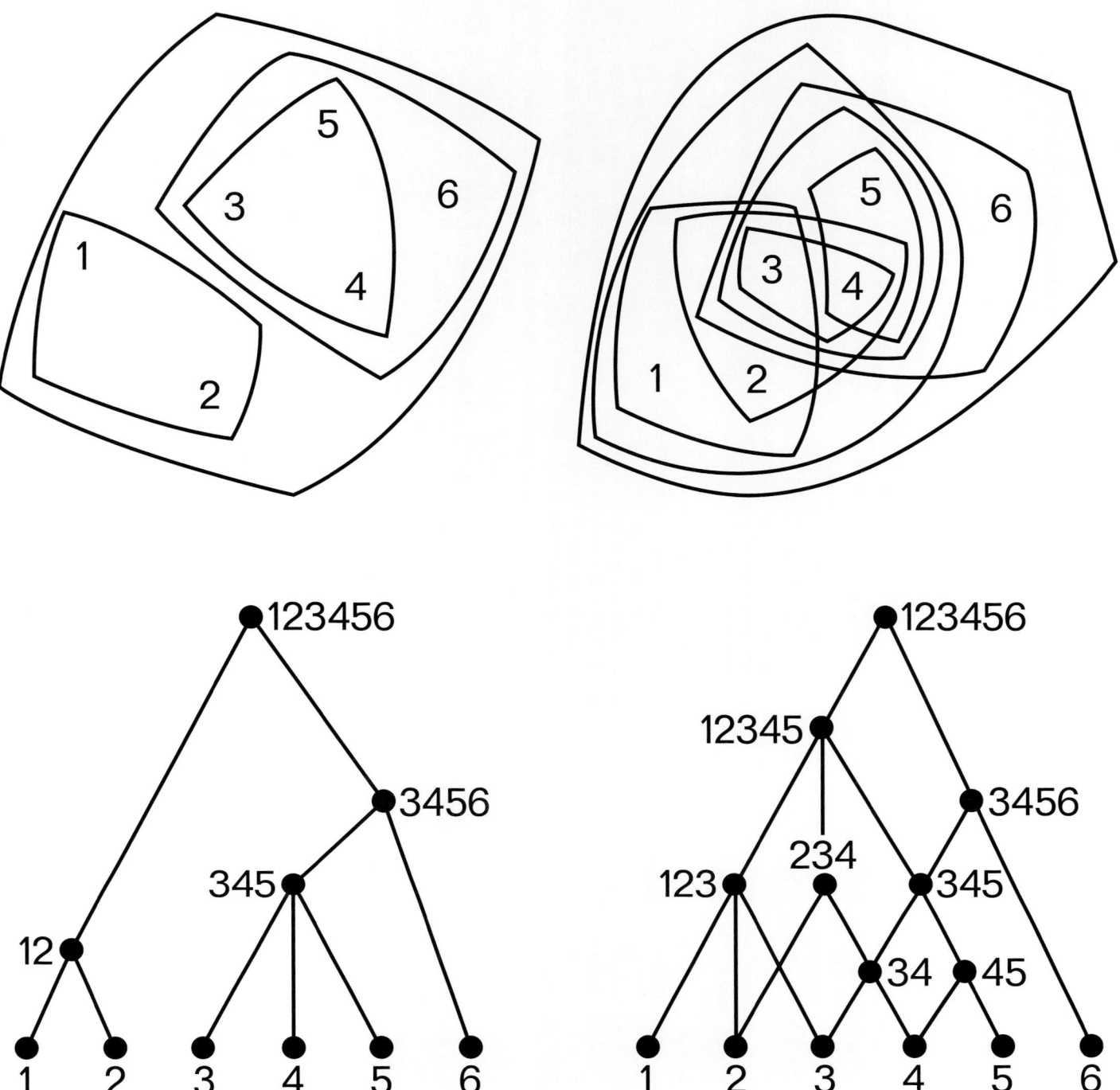

*Redrawn diagram of a semi-lattice (right) and tree structure (left) based
on the work of architect and mathematician Christopher Alexander*

*Source: City is Not a Tree, Christopher Alexander, Architectural Forum,
Vol. 122, No. 1, April 1965, pp. 58–62.*

In his famous 1965 article *A City Is Not a Tree*, architect and mathematician Christopher Alexander criticizes the abstract, tree-like scheme in which each part interacts with the whole through a hierarchical and pyramidal relationship. This top-down model dominated urban planning theory and practice in the decades before and after World War II. In opposition to it Alexander favors the 'natural' city, the one growing organically over time, which resembles a 'semi-lattice': an open structure whose parts are overlapping and cross-connected by different orders of relationships. This model enhances and facilitates multiple connections and informal relationships between different orders of scale and significant interferences between the parts.

Almost six decades after Alexander's article was first published, the tree-model is still clearly recognizable in the design of recently developed new towns, the extension of existing cities and even in rural environments. However, the linear model is extractive rather than regenerative: considering the detrimental effects on the built and natural environment we cannot hold on to this linear model and false sense of stability and predictability. Based on the urgent need to look at relations and interdependencies, , the semi-lattice offers a safer option as a model for resilience.

strategies for change[23] and have created a straightforward color scheme to start identifying them. This simple model can help one to become aware of the position one is taking and also how this differs within a group of people. Even before aligning perspectives, it already helps to start acknowledging the difference between them. In the scheme, producing change through blueprint planning is clearly distinguished from the change produced by the processes of dynamic learning. Reading the descriptions of the different change strategies, there is not much doubt that the latter will serve us better if we want to tackle the wicked problems of environment-making.

This awareness helps to have design in dialogue processes that are capable of addressing contradictions, struggles and uncertainties, and bring together opposing or overlapping perspectives on truth. In the search for this more holistic view, we have to become aware and learn how to deal with asymmetries and incompatibilities between participants and the exclusion and inclusion of stakeholders. Design processes will start to be understood as intervention and integration processes: processes of successive actions to search for shared meaning between participants.

Now what makes this different from how participation processes are often understood nowadays? Design in dialogue it is not just about creating the conditions for everyone to collaborate, but also about creating the ability to actively disrupt, as the necessary condition to transgress boundaries and work in a truly transdisciplinary way. We should not shy away from the continuous assessment this will require. What do we share? What do we make? Who owns what? And who is actually empowered?

A PRACTICE OF PRACTICES

You can see it as a critical facilitation process. A critical facilitator–which we will call an urban transformation facilitator from now on–is a person who increases, manages and organizes complexity, raises critical questions, transcends the various existing perspectives and keeps differences and tensions on the table productively for as long as possible. Ultimately, the urban transformation facilitator guides and stimulates everyone involved in the process to arrive at evermore nuanced choices. Detecting or even activating fields of tension will have to become an integral part of the practice of design in dialogue. It is about addressing the discomfort of dealing with fields of tension and deciding on which ones can be handled to allow meaningful transformations to occur. Despite its sophisticated name, it should be clear that this a role can potentially be taken up by anyone involved. Even more, it is the goal to make it a responsability that is shared by everyone around the table. Each single person contributes to making it possible and carries the resonsibility to think about representation:

who is directly involved in the process and who is (not) represented? It is a situation where you become conscious of how you transform the moment, while also allowing yourself to be transformed by it in turn. Sometimes this even means to take take a step back, or make an extra effort, to create more room around the table for others.

Design can play a role in creating moments of crystallization where these encounters happen. It is in these moments where the magic happens: when different and parallel tracks of transformation and a variety of values become connected and multiple levels of ambition align. Becoming aware of the various perspectives on change and how a transformation process is being conceived is an inherent part of the reflexive action.

The openness to work towards multiple answers has an impact on how we observe, on how we design, and–most importantly–on how we organize ourselves collectively. It is not just a matter of developing a personal sensibility. To be able to shift swiftly and activate one action perspective after another is a matter of a specific collective organization that ties together many different urban practices into a network of collective learning, bundling decision-making and action.

To a certain extent, the diversity of positions to create such an extended practice already exists. The range is there, but remains overlooked as a potential ensemble or open configuration of options. Rather than to discuss whether to produce transformation in this or that way, it seems more fruitful to imagine how it could be done like this *and* like that. And like that. And that. In that sense, design in dialogue and its focus on multiple perspectives is not questioning the value of architectural practices that focus on material value. What it proposes, is to integrate this perspective into a multitude of perspectives and possible outcomes. Only when a design process is handled by a constellation of practices, the collective power to set up a meaningful transformation of our living environment appears.

FACILITATING URBAN TRANSFORMATION

Creating this approach together is crucial. Design in dialogue is not about a fixed methodology, but more about creating a shared understanding and sensibility and about developing a way to think and act together. To be effective, it will require the flexibility to be able to see when to contribute yourself and when it is better to hand over responsibility or activate someone else. Starting from Alexander's understanding of the environment as a series of interlocking patterns, we can start weaving into urban transformation processes different perspectives and ways of *thinking the world* using the thought forms of Laske.

Many different situations require many different actions and it really depends on what you can start from. At times, as happened with Skanderbeg Square, a formal design act can make a difference by setting a common frame to start thinking from. At other times it might be more fruitful to bring people together in an open configuration, freely exchanging and developing ideas. During the temporary occupation of the World Trade Center in Brussels, the investors became increasingly more open to new ideas by being immersed in an environment of difference and dissent. Even if the investors and local activists didn't align or fully agree, their mutual presence created a context that made change more likely, their on multiple fronts. Beyond the immediate results, it is also about creating a culture that is being gradually shaped through such encounters.

Design in dialogue challenges us to see design as an act of giving shape to anything from cities and buildings to the way we work together. To have an expanded view on what can be designed, broadens the scope of the roles and responsibilities of designers and others involved. Instead of a reductionist approach it becomes an open attitude and an expansive practice of practices that understands architecture and urban transformation as an open and dynamic process, propelled by catalytic moments aimed at finding temporary common ground from which common action becomes possible.

This common ground is a moment in time and it is a also a place. Since it is about people, it helps to have environments where they can come together and where concrete encounters can happen. At the various departments at the ETH Zürich, there is a diversity of disciplines and knowledge that creates fertile ground to experiment and reach out beyond the boundaries of disciplines and academia. The Design in Dialogue Lab in Oerlikon, a modest part of town, is set up to become a place for such encounters. It is ambitious and straightforward as a concrete starting point that acknowledges that creating a culture of environment-making will be as much about transforming actual spaces as it will be about creating the conditions for a cooperative social construction.

Freek Persyn[24]

1 – Freek Persyn – was appointed full professor of architecture and urban transformation at the ETH in Zürich on January 1st, 2019, on a 50% basis, combining it with my design practice.

2 In German, the official language at ETH, Architecture and Urban Design translates as *Architektur und Städtebau*

3 *Mirroring effects, Tales of Territory*, Marc Angeil and Carey Siress, p. 867, Ruby Press, 2019

4 As referenced in *Mirroring Effects*, p. 896. Drawing by architect Angelo Bucci entitled *The Thin Layer* depicting the planetary boundary as a shallow zone of approximately 3.5 kilometers that constitutes the inhabitable realm of the Earth; what appears as a single line is actually comprised of two lines, the inner and outer circles of the thin layer.

5 Paola Viganò, *Territories of Urbanism, The project as knowledge producer*, p. 171, EPFL press, Routledge, 2016.

6 In "The city is not a tree" Christopher Alexander critiques the way architects and planners design based on simple mental images like a tree and not based on interesting relationships, like a semi-lattice structure would allow. In 1966, he writes: "It is known today that grouping and categorisation are amongst the most primitive psychological processes. Modern psychology treats thought as a process of fitting new situations into existing slots and pigeon holes in the mind. Just as you cannot put a physical thing into more than one physical pigeon hole at once, so, by analogy, the processes of thought prevent you from putting a mental construct into more than one mental category at once." "A city is not a tree." *Design magazine*, London Council of industrial Design, No. 206, 1966.

7 This way of looking at architecture is closely related to the work of Momoyo Kaijima and Yoshiharu Tsukamoto of Atelier Bow-Wow and their use of the term *'behaviorology'*. In the publication *Atelier Bow-Wow, A primer*, their work is explained as a radicalization of Alexander's work. On p. 100, it is described as such: "Atelier Bow Wow's approach to behaviorology broadens the field of behaviorism in architecture in two respects: it rejects any causal, mono-directional relationship between man and architecture, and it endeavors to apprehend the environment in its entirety as a series of interlinked cycles of cause and effect, in which man, nature and the built environment are all implicated. Behaviorology is accordingly not focused on an isolated event that can be explained in causal or functional terms but rather on a series of events that put all actors–human and non-human–on equal footing." *Atelier Bow-Wow, A primer*, edited by Laurent Stalder, Cornelia Escher, Megumi Komura, Meruro Washida, Verlag der Buchhandlung Walther König, 2013.

8 In 2017, 51N4E moved to the North District in Brussels, an office district that embodies all the traumas of modernist planning. Since its move there, 51N4E has set up and participated in multiple initiatives, in an ongoing experiment to actively engage in the transformation of the neighborhood.

9 The shift proposed here–to see architecture as an act of adaptation rather than as an act of construction–is even taken a step further by Keller Easterling in her essay 'Subtraction'. In this thought-provoking text, she imagines the future challenge of design as one of removal instead of addition. In her words: "For architects, subtraction offers an expanded artistic repertoire of form making as well as a new territory for spatial enterprise and ingenuity." p. 73, *Subtraction, Critical Spatial Practice 4*, Nikolaus Hirsch and Markus Miessen (eds.), Sternberg Press, 2014.

10 A further description of the Saint Nazaire project can be found in the publication *Rewriting Architecture*. The text *Design in Dialogue* elaborates on the process of adaptation, which aimed at shaping a narrative together with future users, from which the architecture followed. p. 179 and following in *Tabula Scripta, Rewriting Architecture*, Floris Alkemade, Michiel van Iersel, Mark Minkjan, Jarrik Ouburg (eds.), Valiz Publishers, 2020.

11 The Kernel of the Way, p. 539, *The Timeless Way of Building*, Christopher Alexander, Oxford University Press, 1979.

12 *The Reflective Practitioner: How Professionals Think in Action.* Donald Schön, Basic Books, 1984.

13 See https://www.51n4e.com/projects/test-site-istanbul. Also, Lars Lerup has been making a similar allusion to being in a state of receptivity in his text on our 50.000 Logements project in Bordeaux: "In this context, much like Buddhists, 51N4E and Grau are deliberately falling into the river (not literally, although the Garonne certainly provides the opportunity). And in turn they swim downstream, which is not traditionally what architects do since they are taught that they know best, so listening is just for courtesy. While floating on their backs, the team members study and take note of the rich ground developed over centuries." 51N4E Double or Nothing, Architectural Association Publications, 2011.

14 For an interesting description of the role of problem-finding in (Swiss) planning processes see: Matthias Loepfe and Angelus Eisinger, "Assemblages for Urban Transformation", *disP - The Planning Review*, 53:1, pp. 20-31, 2017.

15 I was introduced to Otto Laske's Dialectical Thought Form Framework by Jan De Visch, first in the trajectory of the internal redesign of 51N4E's organization, and later in a series of collaborations and subsequent conversations–on projects and initiatives of urban redevelopment and public space design in the region of Flanders.

16 Laske, Otto. *Dialectical Thinking for Integral Leaders, A primer.* Integral Publishers, 2015.

17 A more detailed description of the design process of the Skanderberg Square project can be found on pages 81-92 of the publication *Chapter 1: Skanderberg Square*, Tirana, Ruby Press, 2017.

18 The approach was developed by Fatma Fshazi, at the time also director of the Center of Openness and Dialogue in Tirana, which hosted the model and the dialogue process of the Skanderberg Square in the year 2016.

19 This approach is related to the concerns raised in the *Manifesto for Patchwork Ethnography*: "By patchwork ethnography, we refer to ethnographic processes and protocols designed around short-term field visits, using fragmentary yet rigorous data, and other innovations that resist the fixity, holism, and certainty demanded in the publication process." Günel, Gökçe, Saiba Varma, and Chika Watanabe. 2020. "A Manifesto for Patchwork Ethnography." Member Voices, Fieldsights, June 9. https://culanth.org/fieldsights/a-manifesto-for-patchwork-ethnography.

20 For a more elaborate view on the dialogical approach, see De Visch, J. & Laske, O. (2020) *Practices of Dynamic Collaboration. A Dialogical Approach to Strengthening Collaborative Intelligence in Teams.* Springer, 2020

21 *From Within an Ecology of Practice*, Francesco Garutti introduces The Things Around Us https://www.cca.qc.ca/en/articles/issues/28/with-and-within/73634/from-within-an-ecology-of-practice

22 "Beyond Comparison: Histoire Croisée and the Challenge of Reflexivity", History and Theory, Vol. 45, No. 1, Feb. 2006, pp. 30-50.

23 The color text for change agents helps to ask the question, "How do you think about change?" and has been developed in 2001 by Léon de Caluwé and Hans Vermaak. More information in Dutch: de Caluwé and Vermaak, Leren veranderen: Een handboek voor de veranderkundige, Kluwer, 2006.

24 This text is inspired by the work at 51N4E and our internal discussions with Johan Anrys, Sotiria Kornaropoulou, Dieter Leyssen, among many others. It is constructed using comments and feedback by Jan De Visch of Connect&Transform and it concretely shaped by the comments and insights of Seppe De Blust, Fatma Fshazi. Michiel van Iersel and Charlotte Schaeben, all part of the team at the chair of Architecture and Urban Transformation at the ETH in Zürich. Furthermore, the writing of this text happened in parallel to the making of the exhibition "The Things Around Us" at the CCA in Montreal and was nurtured by the curatorial process there, led by Francesco Garutti and Irene Chin.

New·rope *(nju,rəup)*
The rediscovery of Europe, both as a shared history and a common future, and the exploration of the large diversity of urban practices that inhabit and shape it.

Outline of the idea of 'Newrope' according to the NEWROPE Chair of Architecture and Urban Transformation.

Europe is part of a world that is rebalancing, where the causes and effects of climate change and the exploitation of ecosystems and cities are strongly related to issues of identity, equity and solidarity. Despite, or maybe because of its complex and contested nature and long history of extraction, expansion and exclusion, Europe hosts an array of spatial conditions and democratic practices that can help formulate and answer urgent questions. It offers a fertile test bed to fundamentally rethink urban transformations and social change, finding out how to regenerate rather than to deplete.

In the face of this challenge, the Chair of Architecture and Urban Transformation wants to engage in rediscovering Europe as inhabitable ground, and a shared space for all. This rediscovery of the territory, both as a shared history and a common future, is what we call NEWROPE. It comes with an exploration of the large diversity of urban practices that inhabit and shape Europe.

Credits: NEWROPE, The Design in Dialogue Lab, Chair of Architecture and Urban Transformation, ETH Zürich, Neunbrunnenstrasse 50, 8093, Zürich-Oerlikon, Switzerland. www.newrope.world @newrope.world Art-direction & design: OK-RM

In the second part of this book, we introduce eight projects from eight different practices. Each of them captivates through bold, and at the same time, humble architectural interventions. In individual interviews we asked for the stories behind these outstanding transformations and whether the previously introduced six dimensions of design in dialogue were recurrent as an implicit attitude. We present excerpts of these interviews and give all those involved, the ups and downs and the many dialogues of the projects, the space and due meaning, that are often neglected in favor of clear authorship.

The different interpretations of design in dialogue in each of the projects reveal the personal character of this attitude. All the practices were confronted with specific limitations impacting their projects. To overcome these, they searched for new forms of collaboration or developed specific ways to activate local and embedded knowledge. What at first sight appears to be a common position is often based on conflicting interests and different priorities or values. The practices belong to different professional fields. While some of them engage with all our defined dimensions of design in dialogue, others only touch upon a few.

Part II.

Projects

The Kornhaus stands out. Both from a distance as well as from up close, the granary dominates the the skyline of Zurich. It introduces a whole new scale to the urban context. Also called Swissmill Tower after its operating company, it marks the transition from the residential neighbourhood of Wipkingen to the former industrial quarter, which is increasingly developing into a more mixed, dense and rather exclusive living and working area.

Situated right next to the river Limmat and opposite a public river pool, its 118-meter-high concrete walls rise into the sky. The slender proportions and the iridescent marble-like, grey surfaces lift the weight off the massive structure. It regularly smells of freshly ground grain, almost like pasta shortly after being thrown into boiling water.

How could such an outstanding and purely productive building come about in a city which is under such urban development pressure as Zurich is? How was the project navigated within the city's given, rather rigid framework of urban planning guidelines and public decision-making processes? How could a building, that is not in accordance with the current urban zoning regulations, obtain approval for the necessary development plan?

01 "Considering the height, there were quite different decisive criteria for the engineering: any narrow gap between old and new building structure had to be avoided because of the mice."

Kornhaus Zurich

in conversation with
Veronika Harder and Robert Haas

02 "It was like a doctoral thesis. We had a selective task force of seven scientific professionals working on a solution to control the explosive properties of flour dust. That would have been the killer factor for the whole project."

03   "We only had this one picture. It was the only picture we showed during the whole process. We did not want to start a discussion. This project is already very controversial, we had had enough of discussions."

Out of necessity

"Increasing the size and capacity of the granary in Zürich was a polarizing project. From the beginning we knew we were doing something unusual. We were afraid of the process, because in Switzerland anyone who rejects a new construction can appeal against the building permit within a given period of time. In this case 77 neighbors opposed the plans for the project, which led to a city-wide referendum. We organized an expert group to support us in the first phase, because we became aware that we needed to convince the majority of Zurich's population to vote for a tower of more than a hundred meters. The project transformed into a political process. We spent about two years only for the communication. It was like marketing. Only after a year we could all calm down and talk."

"The building is still being widely discussed and triggers the imagination of people a lot. Above all, the extensive and flat facades invite to fantasize about alternative uses. They come up with thought-provoking ideas, like for example the installation of a climbing wall. Another suggestion that is often raised, is to make the façade green by covering it with plants. It is a nice image , but any moisture infiltration is highly problematic for the production process inside the granary. A single drop of water or a tiny bug would cause major troubles. Definitely benefitting from a grand visual appeal, the structure has however already served as a large canvas. Once Microsoft even organized a projection illuminating the facade."

04   As a precondition for the building permit and in cooperation with 'Grünstadt Zürich', the city's ranger arranged a falcon hatchery on the rooftop of the tower. A live webcam follows the animals displaying their nosedives into the air.

Knowledge of the many

"For two hundred years now, the Kornhaus has been located on this site. Historical drawings show the mill and how the city changed and grew around it over time. Unfortunately, today the whole former industrial neighborhood is being transformed into an area of luxurious apartments and exclusive offices buildings. The city shared with us the feeling of having to counteract this development. They very much appreciated the idea of the mill remaining at its inner-city location. Instead of destroying this industrial heritage, we wanted to strengthen it by reviving the tradition of productive buildings."

"This grain mill is a humongous machine that never stops. It runs 24 hours a day, 365 days a year. We had to ensure that operations could continue without interruption throughout the whole construction process. The knowledge and experience of the employees were essential for this, even more important than the opinion of the engineers. Today, on the tenth anniversary of the bulding's completion, I could look at the building with admiration, but, above all, I remember the people I worked with. One of them is the miller. He might be a bit crazy, but we are still friends!"

Risky experiments

"The competition brief envisaged a grain storage tower of 80 meters. Without any calculation nor permission, we proposed to raise it from 80 to 120 meters. Making it that much higher than requested seemed to be a good idea and we just went for it. At that point, we did not think we would attain that goal and we were confronted with a lot of nasty discussions. The final decision was based on formal and strategic considerations, such as the proportion, the productivity and a balance in the city's skyline. The tower is now three times higher than the original but still a few meters lower than the 126-meter Primetower. We didn't want to tread on the toes of Zurich's architects too much here."

Kornhaus, Zurich

06   "Every child who looks at these pictures knows what is inside. There is no need for explanation, it is an archetypical form."

Design in dialogue

  05   "After winning the competition, we had to warn the owner, that if the neighbors wouldn't agree, we wouldn't be able to build the tower as high as envisaged."

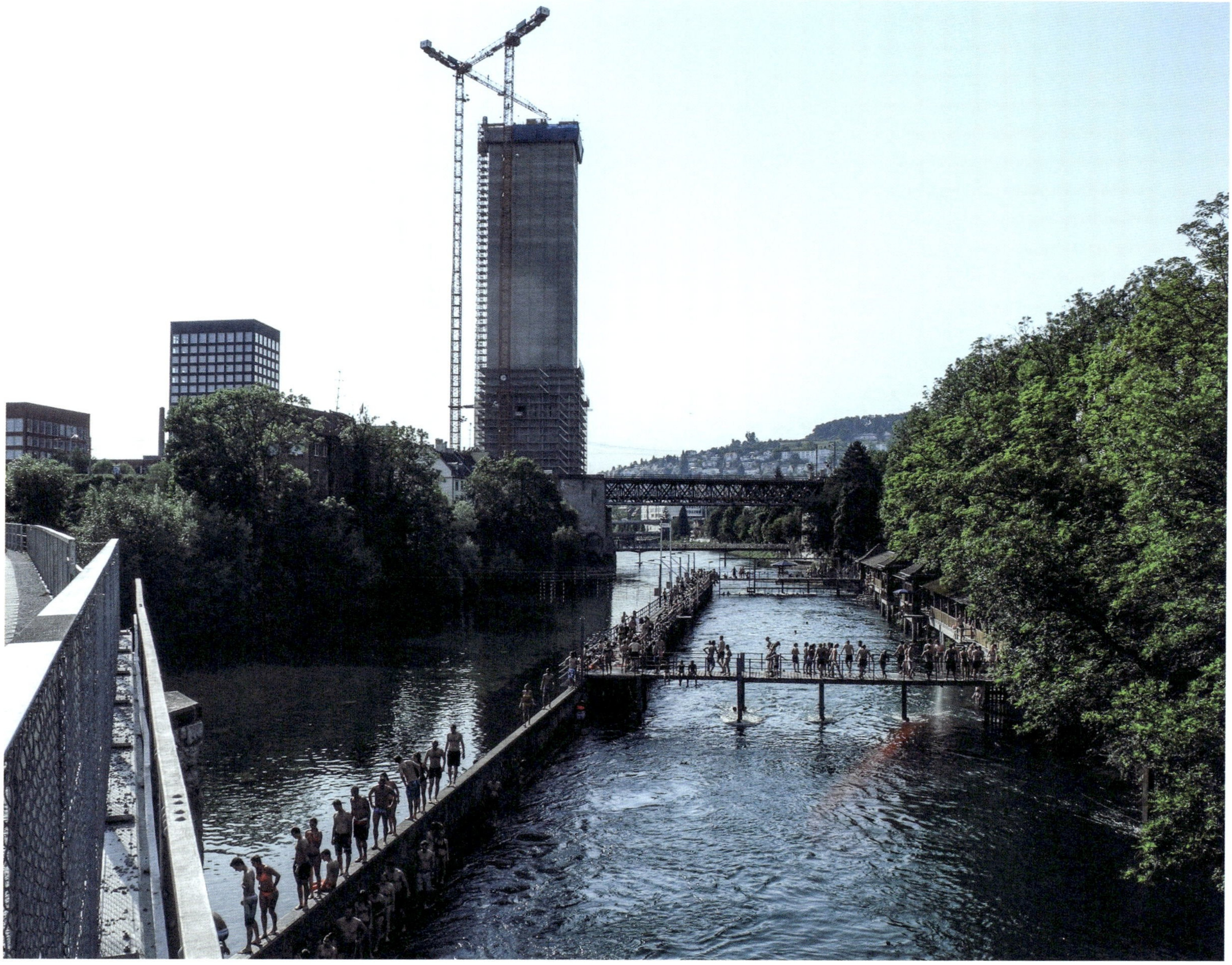

07 “It’s a project of increasing the existing mill. Today the building reaches up 120 meters and at the same time descends 40 meters underground.”

Safe ground for learning

“The design is based on Corbusier’s ‘The engineer as designer’. The typology and construction method with ‘Gleitbeton’ defined the way we work. You do not have a lot of formal possibilities and you have to be creative within the given constraints. Understanding what we are doing based on the process of construction, is very important for us and forms our space for discussion.”

“Semantics matter a lot to us. We nicknamed the building ‘Kornhaus’, which means ‘house of grain’. In German, it is a historical term and almost has the connotation of a brand. We prefer this name to the word ‘Silo’, because in this purely industrial term the social and human component is lost. The Kornhaus, on the contrary, is something that provides us with our daily food and is thus much closer to our daily lives and to us as citizens and humans.”

Senior improvisor

“We gave many presentations, guided visits and did a lot of political work. We were speaking, speaking, speaking. Together with our client’s communication office, we built a campaign of which most of the strategy derived from the main slogan: This is our daily bread. In Zurich, people, especially elderly people, are religious. Their main prayer is ‘Vater unser, gib uns unser täglich Brot’, which somehow already shows the importance of the grain. People really enjoy their ‘Muesli’, ‘Gipfeli’, and ‘Brot’, which are firmly anchored in Swiss culinary culture. Nowadays, complex production and distribution networks are harming this direct relationship to food. We wanted to emphasize this local production, so we brought bread every time we met with others. Even at the building committee, we always brought freshly baked bread to share.”

Silogegner sünnelen im Badedress

ZÜRICH. Brrrrr – trotz Temperaturen nur knapp über dem Gefrierpunkt haben am Samstag Dutzende in Badehosen und Bikini den Paradeplatz bevölkert und ihn kurzerhand zur Badi umfunktioniert. Damit warben sie für ein Nein zum Swissmill-Silo, über den die Stadtzürcher am 13. Februar abstimmen. Der 120-Meter-Turm würde die Untere-Letten-Badi zeitweise in den Schatten stellen.

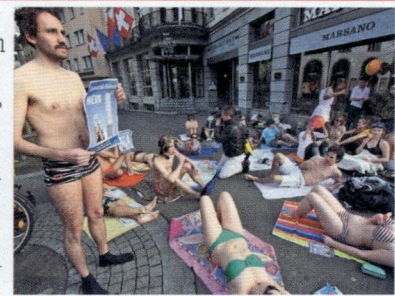

08 “One of the main discussion points was the shadow of the building. We had to prove that it would not overshadow the river pool until six o’clock in the evening.”

Collectively rethinking social housing for the 17th arrondissement in Paris was the goal of the 'Grand Projet de renouvellement urbain de la porte Pouchet'. Paris Habitat, the project's developer and key actor in the city's social housing, invited nine young international offices to design solutions for a 600-meter-long and 12-meter-wide strip of land that had been reclaimed from the existing road network. Atelier Bow-Wow's contribution is characterized by its generosity in public space paired with a detailed, clear and open architectural form. In an area characterized by large housing estates and no urban core, the aim was to recreate commonalities. By setting back the building, the public street space for pedestrians was to be expanded and the external quality of the ground floor was to be improved through the specific and precise use of integrated public furniture. With its claimed ambition to always respond to the environment and the needs of the users, Atelier Bow-Wow also sought answers to the question of flexibility, adaptability and repetition in the architectural expression and interior.

How did this careful translation of ideologies from the usual context from Japanese cities to Paris succeed? How can functional, user-friendly and everyday living space be designed for an unknown and diverse group of inhabitants? Which role did the reflection on classic local typologies play in this?

Rue Rebière
Paris

in conversation with
Momoyo Kaijima
and Yoshiharu Tsukamoto

09   "We just try to keep on talking, talking, talking and then go back to the beginning, to the reason why we are doing this. What is the meaning of the project, not just of that part? If then one part, one detail, one element becomes a subject for debate, we go back to the overall ideas of the project."

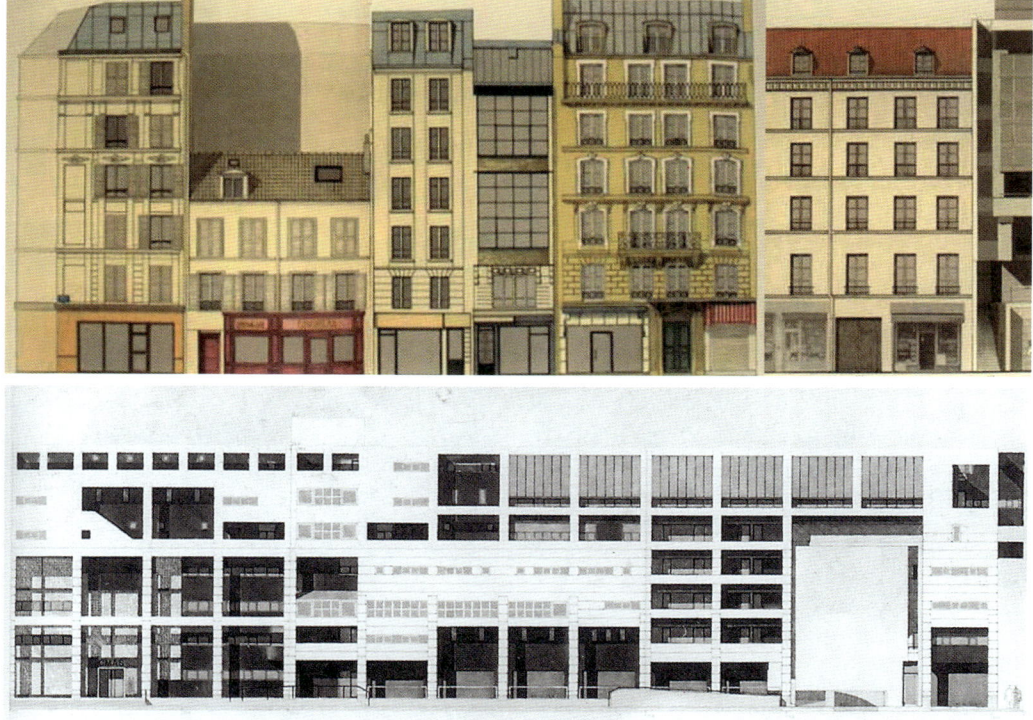

10   "Modernist apartments are based on the idea of flexibility, but this dream is difficult in practice. So, I think housing typology works better with the idea of redundancy, instead of flexibility."

Out of necessity

"The moment I left Tokyo was a moment of an economic bubble. Its architectural design scene was that of extravaganza. Any kind of newness was appreciated, but for me most of the designs were rather shabby. Also in Europe, I really enjoyed visiting many interesting buildings, but I never felt involved. This impression made me very sad. So since then, for me being involved is a very important value in architecture. My studies in Paris were far more discipline oriented, approaching the profile of a street, the city's morphology and architectural typology as an integrated whole. This is something we totally lost in Japan. Rue Rebière, a street in the 17th arrondissement of Paris, is an area without strict regulation about the beauty of buildings. Nine architects, six French, one Swiss and us from Japan joined the project. Some really wanted to show their ability, their design vocabulary and originality. We were more looking for consistency."

11-12   "I was involved in the studio directed by Ciriani, a leader of a teaching group called 'Uno'. Uno is a group of professors who believe in Corbusier's principles. The professor always asked students to read every night before going to bed. I was quite shocked at the beginning, but after one month I started to realize that this way of studying architecture was very helpful for me in that moment."

13   "The repetition of the French window allows you to make tiny little studios with one window and huge apartments over two storeys and ten windows."

"When we design a single-family house, we are interested in the personal routines, habits or even cooking preferences of the family. At Rue Rebière we had to design for the uncertain. Collective housing requires a broader understanding of how people live in spaces. Especially in a foreign context. A strong urban canon given from the city with its historical and cultural references, with classic typologies, like the French window, becomes very important. Why were these repeated so much? We can summon the people from 1900, that passed away, through the typology, but at the same time we were summoned by typology."

14   "Wood is often preferred as a building material because of its warmer atmosphere, but clients are concerned about the budget for maintenance and generally respond to this idea with a firm 'no'."

Safe ground for learning

"In the design process, one mostly encounters rejection at some point. We are very interested in this 'no'. Why does someone say 'no'? The general rejection often conceals certain concerns, personal bad experiences, a lot of smaller no's. Those need to be broken down one by one. A frequent example is the criticism of excessively high maintenance costs. Often, they can be anticipated by prioritizing them from the start of a project. We try to engage through a bottom-up way of thinking, to understand what everybody needs and wants. This process, what we call 'sounding', becomes the form and erases the worries. This feedback loop is the core method of our design. Of course, it takes a lot of time, a lot of consideration—but somehow, it is also fun."

15   "Typology-wise social housing is very fixed and standardized. The ceiling height is set to 2.5 meters, the floor plan is regulated by the number of bedrooms, and each room has its standards. Any violation becomes extremely expensive."

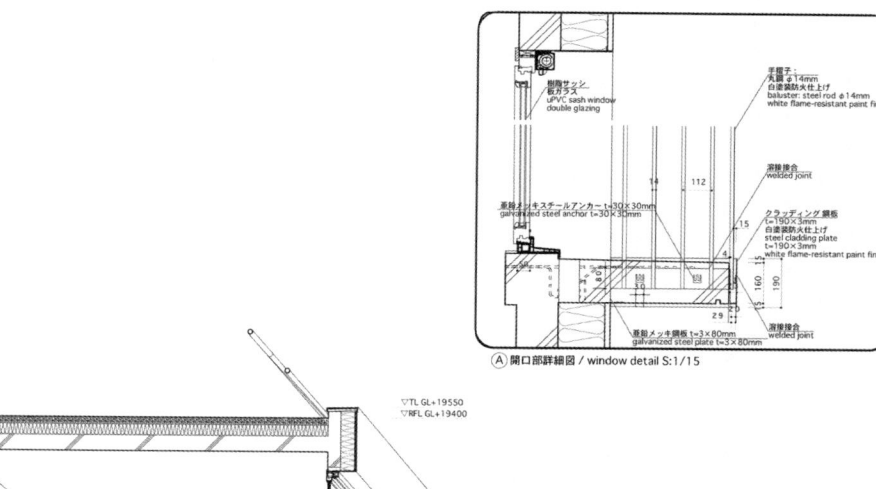

(A) 開口部詳細図 / window detail S:1/15

uPVC sash window
double glazing

樹脂サッシ
防水ガラス

baluster: steel rod φ14mm
white flame-resistant paint finish

手摺子／
大麗 φ14mm
白塗装耐火仕上げ

welded joint

溶接接合

galvanized steel anchor t=30×30mm

亜鉛メッキスチールアンカー t=30×30mm

cladding: steel cladding plate
t=190×3mm
white flame-resistant paint finish

クラッディング 鋼板
t=190×3mm
白塗装耐火仕上げ

galvanized steel plate t=3×80mm

亜鉛メッキ鋼板 t=3×80mm

welded joint

溶接接合

▽TL GL+19550
▽RFL GL+19400

断面詳細パース / vertical section perspective S:1/50

Loggements Sociaux Rue Rebière

Senior improvisor

"With its set-back facade and a loggia on the ground level, we proposed to expand the public street space. We wanted to have an integrated bench next to the entrance in this loggia. The local collaborators were quite afraid of this idea because of vandalism. They said: 'No, no, no, no!'. I eased their minds, explaining this set-up is okay, because vandalism happens when it is hidden from the street. Then our French partner gave a radio interview where he argued for the generosity of public open spaces, and how it used to be planned in the 1970s. The very next day, Paris Habitat gave in. They made a phone call and the permission for the bench was granted. They were suddenly convinced of the importance of this detail, which they until then had considered as formally irrelevant."

Culture of cooperation

"The two of us studied at the same laboratory in Tokyo Tech. At that time, Yoshi was a doctoral student and I was a master's student, and we spent time together and had interesting conversations. By starting to collectively design, test and investigate on a more academic level, we gained knowledge on how to communicate between different contexts. The three approaches of practice, research and experimentation through teaching or building installations became more and more related. Looping these three different positions, to combine them with each other is what we call 'transduction'. This art of transduction finds its framework in the working environment of the laboratory. Here, the internal transfer of experience and knowledge is as important as representing the interests of society."

16   "We are very interested in how to express our experiences in drawings. We therefore collect all the material we work with regarding scale, details and process and bring them into anatomic drawings."

17 "We became involved as neighbors. Some of us were living there, some of us working so many hours that it was almost like living in the neighborhood."

La Borda Barcelona

in conversation with
Cristina Gamboa

It is the image of an incredibly spacious, open, collective and undefined space that makes one curious about the project La Borda. The housing cooperative was created as part of the Can Batlló social movement, a community driven process aiming at the recovery of the industrial premises in the Sants neighborhood of Barcelona. As part of this platform a group of young architects came together within the scope of their master's thesis at the Technical University. Being confronted with a highly speculative real estate market of a city in the midst of a welfare crisis, the aim was to think about a new model of collective housing. The project, which began as a student project, institutionalized itself step by step. Initially engaged as investigators, then as neighbors and activists, the architects formed the cooperative LACOL, where some even became part of the process as end users. Three fundamental and cross-sectional principles are defining the project: redefining the collective housing program, sustainability and environmental quality and user participation.

How was the project embedded in the greater dynamics of the whole neighborhood? How were the shared values communicated while leaving enough space for the development of the project considering its individual users? How could a strong architectural concept be combined with such multi-layered participatory processes?

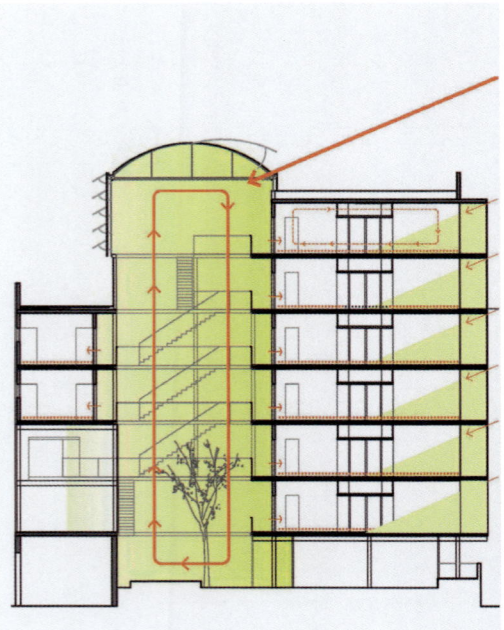

18 "I think that for us the first thing was to acknowledge people. If you don't have the information to decide, it makes no sense for us to discuss the architecture of the project. Nowadays all the members can explain the project in the same way we could."

"Can Batlló was one of the biggest former industrial areas of Barcelona, waiting to be transformed. The citizens of the neighborhood founded an initiative for its collective transformation, aiming to create more spaces for leisure and cultural activities. We realized that different needs were present in the neighborhood, and one of these was housing. Remember, this was in 2011 and 2012, in the middle of the crisis. The idea was to introduce new domestic space, a new model of housing totally based on a non-speculative mode of development, to break away from the idea of individual ownership."

19 "Before La Borda there were three empty houses squatted by really vulnerable people. As most of us were involved in housing activism, it was a huge contradiction to evict people from the plot that the municipality offered us. I think this is part of being aware what it means to develop the neighborhood, that there is always a pre-existing condition and contradictions you have to deal with."

20 "I think that this image reflects a lot about the project, because next to the main values of conviviality, a political and non-speculative moral, we tried to be very sustainable regarding resources. From that moment on, when La Borda realized that it was political to develop a sustainable building, we got involved with really experienced consultants and teachers."

21 "Can Batlló is a neighborhood with a tradition of cooperatives, social movements and civic networks. In the moment we started to be engaged there was a general discussion on how neighborhood organizations could be dealing with the needs created by the welfare crisis."

Safe ground for learning

"Once we had to decide about our master's project at the university, we were looking for spaces in the neighborhood that could work as a case study. The idea was to become part of the activities of Can Batlló by investigating the opportunity to develop a cooperative housing project in an existing building or on an empty plot. Over time and by presenting the project to a growing audience, the project became reality. The cooperative La Borda was set up and Lacol evolved towards a non-profit cooperative of architects."

"The future residents were involved in the construction process from the very beginning. The working groups and monthly meetings were less about curated participation than a direct exchange of knowledge. We collectively discussed all the data of the financial calculations, structural engineering, environmental issues, and how they influenced the project in terms of architecture. In order to collect this knowledge and keep the decisions retraceable, we set up a manual to provide insights of prior workshops and debates. Another tool is the live monitoring of six flats, where we record parameters like CO_2 concentration or humidity to produce protocols of use in winter and summer."

Knowledge of the many

"Understanding the neighborhood was important to define our program. For example, we had public libraries in the neighborhood and study spaces in Can Batlló, so we do not have a library in the building. But we have a guest room, for temporary housing or visitors of workshops or international meetings happening in the neighborhood. It is like a community inside a community. It is not an island or isolated project. The neighborhood scale is also crucial for the urban strategy. We have this open ground floor, which allows people to cross our building on an existing street. There is a cooperative shop on the ground floor, as a piece of the larger puzzle. It was important for us to understand which kind of facade, activity and relationship we wanted to have with the surrounding area."

22–23 "We had a super-low budget, which triggered a lot of discussions about what to do. We focused on the values of the project and the priorities more than on specific details of construction."

25–26 "We didn't build for a specific number of residents from the beginning onwards. We started with fourteen units. Once we had an agreement with the municipality about the plot, we opened the group to 28 units. The architecture also mainly defined the number of residents, taking into account a comfortable ratio between common space and private flats."

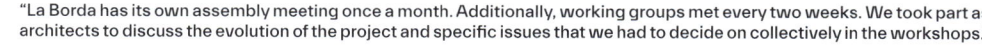

24 "La Borda has its own assembly meeting once a month. Additionally, working groups met every two weeks. We took part as architects to discuss the evolution of the project and specific issues that we had to decide on collectively in the workshops."

Senior improvisor

"The main strategies, the program, the model of conviviality and the sustainability goals were decided on collectively. However, La Borda is a cooperative of users. You are not the owner, so we cannot totally design the flats based on the needs of one specific user. We defined the building as an infrastructure. That means that we designed temporary tools and furniture, as the kitchen for example, in such an adaptive way that we could reconfigure it for future users."

Culture of cooperation

"In order to allow the experiences and knowledge of collective processes to become visible, shared and supportive to other groups, the platform of exchange, La Dinamo, was founded. It is a foundation that we have been working on that tries to implement and replicate cooperative housing and give support to administrations and private developers. It is a kind of umbrella organization promoting and developing social and cooperative housing. In the end, La Borda had a lasting impact on the whole city of Barcelona, who introduced parts of our approach into its new housing plan. What is important is that we understand in which way these processes are replicable, to give support to other groups. I think each social group is a different world and you have to be really flexible and adaptable to understand the needs of the group. There is no fixed and unique methodology."

27   "I think that the very good dialogue with the engineer is visible in the project. Bernardo, who is very passionate about boats and sailing, gave a first hint to use a principle similar to those of the sails. Now, there are a lot of things that try to give the space a bit of rigidity, and finally, it worked."

Theaterplein Antwerp

in conversation with
Paola Viganò

A large, lofty porch was selected as the winner of an international competition for the Theaterplein in Antwerp. The proposal conquered minds and hearts by carefully balancing monumentality and lightness. Seeming like little more than a light roof on high, slender stilts over a generous public open space, the design creates a cube-like space. It frames the previously unfathomable and undefined expanse of the square. This straightforward and filigree intervention improves the experience of existing users, while at the same time opening up new possibilities. The weekly market and the previously unwelcome skaters have been given their appropriate space and shelter from rain and sun, while as a café and garden the space also invites new users to stay and linger around the area. The square is an urban stage offering many different opportunities. It sends out an open invitation and is ready to be filled with life, play and movement. It took the people of Antwerp some time to acknowledge this open invitation and imagine new ways to use the infrastructure, but the theater and the Theaterplein have become a central, bustling hub in the heart of Antwerp.

What were the underlying thoughts and principles behind the decision to leave the square as such vacant? How could the desolate state of the surroundings spark such imagination? And how does one succeed in sharing such a nuanced idea of a space and open it up to others?

28 "So, in terms of dialogue, I have to say, I use a different word: conversation. For me and for us, a project is a conversation with an existing situation."

29 "I think one of the best compliments we received for that square came from the mayor. He said: 'I'm very pleased with the result, because I had only commissioned a new square, but everybody has the impression that I have built a new theater!'"

Out of necessity

"The fact that the building's facade had been visually ruined by two red metal emergency stairs earlier on, illustrates to what extent the concrete aesthetic from the 1970s was met with criticism by previous generations. As in many places, concrete was not really regarded as a finishing material. As a consequence, the theater was perceived as ugly. The square in front was not used a lot, except by skaters, who had badly affected the pavement. Only on Saturdays and Sundays, weekly markets temporarily transformed the square into an attractive public space. Throughout the week, the vast dimensions were not an asset. It was just a vast, empty place. With the fundamental idea of public space never being generous enough, this big emptiness needed to be articulated while maintaining the flexibility for existing uses."

"The vision of designing a theatrical space is based on an imaginary engagement with the site and its possible future users, such as performers, dancers and children. It really should be a playground that only acquires its meaning through its use as a stage. In contrast to a dialogue that thrives on mutual responses, this is more of an imaginary conversation. It is triggered by a conceptual design that comes to resonate only after a long time. It generates new images, beyond what the site is immediately communicating. And, nevertheless, these new images are the very things that we imagine that should be, or become reality. There is this relationship between the 'to be' and the 'must be'. And in the end, there probably will be more than what you have imagined in the first place. This is exactly the case at the Theaterplein."

Knowledge of the many

"Any situation is spatial, social, political and economic. The conversation with a site is not only one with the physical context. It is also a conversation with references, with imageries. This project originated out of an imaginary conversation with one of my PhD mentors and Bernardo Secchi's colleague at IUAV in Venice: Gianugo Polesello. It is a composition of some pure space, a big cube, some lines. In that sense, it is a conceptual project, proposing a conceptual space, which does not mean that there is not a deep attention to the context. Is this something that is not taking care of reality? No, absolutely not. It is, on the contrary, a concept of space which is adequate to that situation, able to receive the market and many different practices."

30 "Recently, because sometimes, I see some new images of the square appearing, I saw that there was a performance of the movie 'Dogville' on the square. If you are a dancer there, on that space, you really want to move, no, to dance."

"Composition has something to do with literature, with arts, with music. As a music composer, you compose with space. The space of the square of Theaterplein was too big. It needed to be defined differently and one way was through a cube of air with a roof. This decision was the result of an imaginary conversation with Polesello, a kind of implicit homage to his teaching. As the structure of the architectural competitions does not really allow space for exchange, this discussion was purely an internal one. In this case it was a good thing, because we were not aware of the difficulties of building such a 24-meter-high space above an existing underground parking lot."

31   "The garden was conceived as a thick sponge, a place that welcomes people and invites them to lounge around in a less exposed way. It also retains the rain water from the rest of the square."

Safe ground for learning

"The garden is created as a complementary space, in which people can rest. It introduces a dimension of everyday use, which is radically different from the scenographically designed square. We needed quite some time to understand exactly where we wanted to go with the idea of the garden, and I think the city needed time to understand what to do with this space. In the end, three main elements were used: the rhythm of the neighboring building structure, apple trees for the white color of the flowers and a soft ground vegetation. Today, the garden is used as a terrace, as an urban living room and really acts as a necessary and pleasant counterpart to the hard paving of the square."

32   "Markets are always very precious in the city. When you have a market, you have to do everything to maintain it. There is no discussion on that."

33   "The two themes, the territorial system of parks connecting to the river Scheldt and the theme of porosity of Theaterplein were fundamental to our thinking about the structural plan of Antwerp."

34   "We go to Antwerp? Antwerp—yes, the Flemish painters! I think that when you go on the site, you go with all this imagery that you bring with you. Sometimes this is helpful, sometimes not."

Senior improvisor

"From the very beginning on, the greater ambition was to create a new agenda for urbanism and the urban project. The main point was to work on the relationship between architecture and urbanism, between the architectural project and the true masterplan. We wanted to blur the boundaries between these areas. Those boundaries had become increasingly rigid. The planner was someone who, without drawings and drafts, increasingly lost understanding of the spatial project and the architect, who remained more and more bound to a small plot, neglected the confrontation with the urban scale. The city of Antwerp brought the necessary conditions to test our set of instruments. We had thought it through, and we were ready, but confronted with a new context to understand. And of course, we didn't speak Dutch. Talking about dialogue, this made us feel a bit cut off. We needed to be very attentive to all other signals, to use all our senses to detect whatever appeared to be important."

35   "Polesello was a very abstract, conceptual designer. His designs are very clean, containing nothing more than what is needed. He made beautiful sketches and models, radiating a deep understanding of composition."

Culture of cooperation

"When I share this story, I speak of it in the terms of a of love story. It was so perfect. It was a project that combined working on the small, local sale of the square and on the big scale: the structural plan of Antwerp. It truly was a dream coming true!"

Instead of an answer to the competition brief about the transformation of the main intersection Les Glòries in Barcelona, the many authors of the project Altres Glòries decided to ask questions. Questions about today's role and responsibility of architecture and urban planning and what alternative future scenarios for Barcelona, a city suffering from heavy motorized traffic and decreasing air quality, could look like. In a consortium of eleven offices visions were formulated that questioned the decisions that were already made. Instead of accepting an extensive tunnel construction as a given starting point for the design to be submitted, Altres Glòries proposes to invest the available funds differently. They created a framework that would allow the project to adapt to changing conditions and to introduce new ecological infrastructures for a more sustainable, greener, fairer city, leaving space and time for an evolving design by future generations.

How could so many people agree to free themselves from the production pressure of a competition and submit such a radical and speculative proposal? How can one ensure a continuous critical discussion and at the same time visualize it? How can valuable oral discussion be shared and communicated?

Altres Glòries Barcelona

in conversation with
Pere Buil and Roger Tudó

36 "The project of Glòries was for us a way to discuss the city, the urban morphology. Since we were with eleven offices to make a proposal, the whole process was more a team dialogue, a reflection in an abstract way about what the city should be."

37–38   "I think we all learned to have an open perspective on design, and for example use trees and timing as tools for intervention."

Out of necessity

"The group of Altres Glòries was originally formed during an exhibition called 'A sensitive Matter — Young Catalan Architects', that I curated a few years before. I asked ten young offices in Catalonia to participate, because they had a common approach to architecture during the financial crisis. We invited guest critics from the different places we travelled to, and for all of us these were moments to grow and learn from others. When the competition of Glòries appeared, I asked them if they wanted to team-up. It seemed to me the perfect occasion to discuss how we think about the city, on another, larger scale."

"Glòries, designed as one of the most important squares of the Cerdà Plan, has never been treated as such. The city council decided to demolish the existing infrastructure from the 1980s, an elevated ring of circulation with a parking underneath, and to replace it with a tunnel. That was the starting point for the competition. One thing that we disliked about the brief was that a lot of things were already decided upon, which we thought needed to be questioned. Our proposal consisted of using the money needed for the tunnel to buy adjacent private land in order to avoid housing speculation. It was aimed at reducing traffic, limiting construction exclusively to social housing and gaining generous public space."

PLAÇA DE LES GLÒRIES. FEBRER 2009

39   "The decision to demolish the roundabout was the result of a participatory approach by the public. Although this may not have been a good idea, it had already been decided."

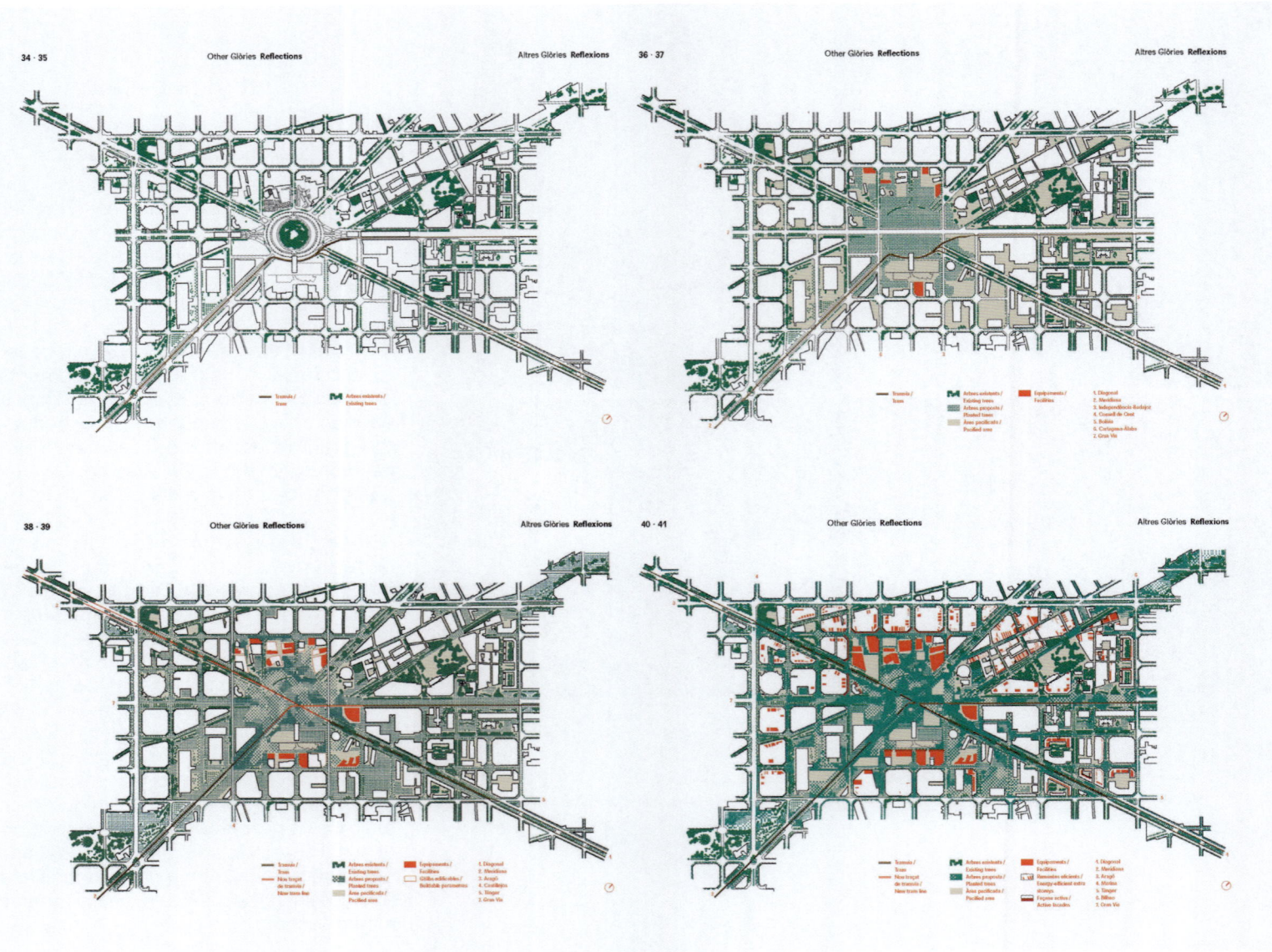

40   "The process led us to decide that the space had to be something evolving, designed over time by the users. In order to facilitate this, we made a plantation plan consisting of trees that grow very fast in three years. This would give the space the shadow needed for direct use."

Safe ground for learning

"We decided that in order to reduce the influence of everybody, it was very important to have a neutral space that was not the office of anybody. In there, a 'production team' of four people, of whom three were students, worked on the project around the clock, without the influence of any of the offices. All eleven offices met only once a week to discuss and debate. The space was an unused, centrally located art gallery in Raval near the Museum of Contemporary Art. It was easily accessible for everyone and offered enough space for the large meetings of the whole team and for model building."

"The fact of not making drawings, not picking up a pencil, but only collectively discussing the work of the production team once a week, was a challenge for some of the offices. A lot of times we had drawings on the wall, but the discussion was not about the drawings, it was about the discussion. I think it is necessary in this kind of process to have somebody that is not focused on design, but on a kind of organizational structure, to produce changes. I think we did not develop this enough. We had this kind of agenda, a lot of people around us from different disciplines, but I think we probably should have had somebody focusing on producing evolution in the activity."

Knowledge of the many

"This project is a collective effort. All the participating offices should be in the credits, in one block, as one, single author and in alphabetical order: Bosch.capdeferro, Josep Bunyesc, Francisco Cifuentes, Data AE, Harquitectes, Emiliano López, Mònica Rivera, Núria Salvadó, David Sabastian, Ted'A, Unparell d'arquitectes and Vora."

Senior improvisor

"With the payment of 20,000 Euro in the final round of the competition, we started to discuss how we would use it. Until then, all of us, except the production team had worked on a voluntary basis. We felt like that it was nice to have a register of the proposal and our common process and decided to invest the money in a book. Bizarrely enough, or as a result of our collective effort, we previously made the decision to record all our meetings and collect all the material of the projects in folders ordered by day. This created the perfect record to start composing our publication."

41   "'Matèria Sensible' was an exhibition and an opportunity to get to know each other. As young Catalan offices we were brought together because of our common approach to architecture in the moment of change back then, when the crisis started."

42   "We did not have the idea of making the book from the beginning, but we somehow knew that we were doing something special, something important in our career."

43   "It was really important during the final moments to have empathy with everybody. We worked with a very young and non-professional team, some of whom were still at the university."

Culture of cooperation

"What we could understand from the jury was that our proposal was clearly not going to win, because it was too abstract and too removed from what they were asking. But it was also very important for them and weighted in the decision on the selection. Even after the competition, there were presentations organized around the selected proposal. We were always invited to these discussions because our proposal was the most radical. Now it looks much more standard, but ten years ago in Barcelona, it was quite strong."

The energy of Onkruid is contagious. All these years they managed to challenge architects from all over the world to travel to a small castle in a rural area near Leuven and design an ideal stage for their festival of dreams: Horst. Today, the group has reached a turning point. They had to relocate the festival and landed in more urban area, on the border of Brussels.

ASIAT is a former military site in the north of Vilvoorde that was abandoned sometime in 2012. In late 2018 the city of Vilvoorde managed to acquire the ground in its totality and began facing the challenge of finding a suitable development strategy. In collaboration with 51N4E and Plant en Houtgoed, Onkruid won a call for proposals to design and build interventions to facilitate temporary use and occupation by events and a summer program.

Onkruid has the ambition to settle at ASIAT, take responsibility and manage a site for ten years. Also, they want to experiment with what could be considered as an infinite festival. This does something to the group. How do you work closely together for such a long time? How do you manage to preserve your artistic freedom? And who do you invite to dance along?

ASIAT Vilvoorde

in conversation with
Mattias Staelens

44   "When designing for the unpredictable, dialogue needs to start before design. And not with one person, but with ten or twenty people."

Out of necessity

"Horst is an annual event we have been working on for five years. The main ambition was to create a unique experience by organizing a festival bringing different artistic disciplines together. The festival was organized on a cultural heritage site near Leuven, which raised the question of how to permanently change such a place. Can a festival be combined with an exhibition? And what possibilities arise when the design of the exhibition turns into a permanent intervention? Now that we moved to the Asiat site in Vilvoorde this logic changed. The place is longing for long term transformation. Raising the question of what you want to leave behind shifts from a condition to an objective."

ASIAT, Vilvoorde

45   "ASIAT was never a plan within our future perspective. But all of a sudden it was an opportunity. A military domain of six hectare where there is a kind of village with a city feeling. Twenty sheds, but also an officers' bar, a boiler room that functions as a church in a village. The whole village is overgrown because it has been empty for twenty years. This has given it a romantic, green feel."

"Working on the Asiat site shifted the perspective. We had to organize a space where everyone is invited to participate and realize their own projects. This noble idea is challenging. Unexpected questions popped up all the time. Do we want a local crochet artist to transform the trees next to our stages? The desire to make people's ideas heard, together with time pressure and stress, led to frustrating situations and the feeling of continuously being late. This made us understand that we need to engage with design in dialogue on a next level, way earlier in the process."

Design in dialogue

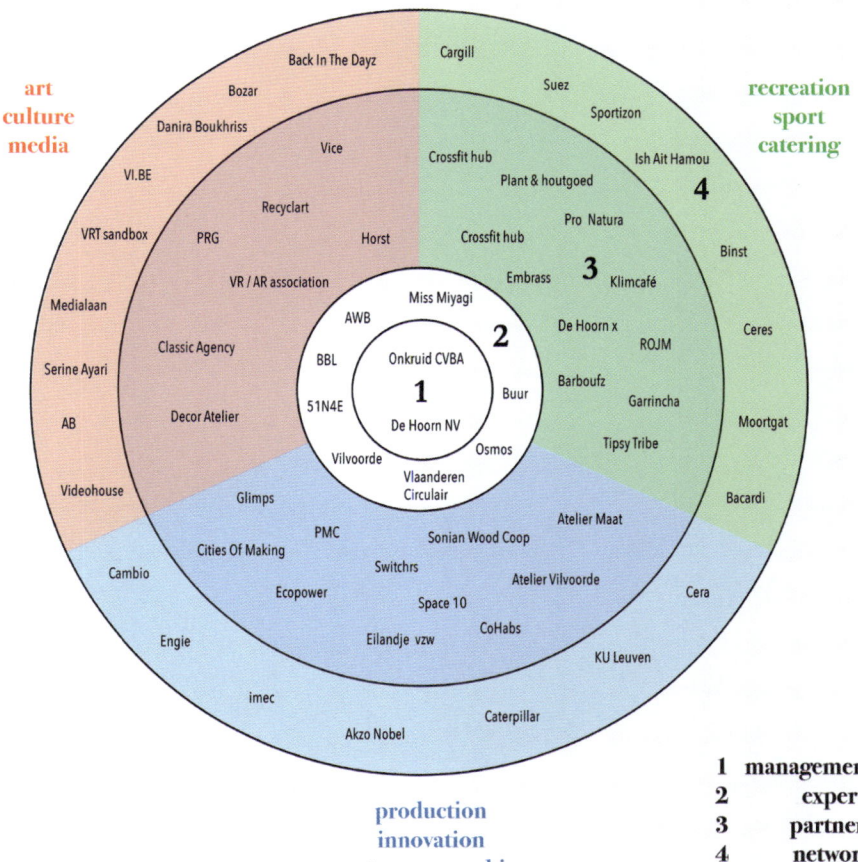

1   management
2   experts
3   partners
4   network

46   "Organizing a festival for multiple years made us experienced in dealing with surprises. We search for this surprise; it is almost a fundamental part of our attitude. In both our projects and our collaborations, we see ourselves as facilitators of a much broader ecosystem."

47–48 "The site of Asiat was recently bought by the city of Vilvoorde with the ambition to develop public facilities but without a clear strategy or means. It became an opportunity for us as an office to explore new directions."

Knowledge of the many

"In contrast to Horst, where a coherent and focused program was developed, we needed to design for a wide and flexible use by unknown parties at ASIAT. At Horst, the visual, the architectural and the artistic were very important. At ASIAT on the other hand, very practical concerns steered the design process. Combining both is a challenge. A stage that worked very well for the Horst music festival does not automatically create the right conditions for a broader program."

Safe ground for learning

"Based on our experience during the first year, we decided to proactively organize and facilitate conversation. This year we are building a pavilion together with Leopold Banchini, that will literally become a place for dialogue: on the one hand for talks programmed by Horst, and on the other hand for dialogues between Horst and local associations. For us it is a way to present ourselves, what we do on the site and ask local organizations and individuals how they want to engage. By having this conversation, which is completely off-limits for us, we might find new ways to program our festival and exhibition, so it fits multiple purposes."

49–50 "Last year we built a pavilion with Fala atelier, which was an intimate outdoor space used as an auditorium or for screenings, yoga etc. In the end we allowed a football team to open a bar there. When they lost interest again, we realized that designing something for an unknown use becomes much more difficult, unpredictable even."

51 "In our program, we strongly steer functional requirements, less the visual ones. Horst-ASIAT is a spatial-artistic experiment. We also want to ensure this in our collaboration with international architects and visual artists."

Senior improvisor

"It is important and almost a contradiction that we try to combine the strategy of a festival with temporary occupation. If the festival is successful, the site will become more attractive, more people will start to occupy it leading to less space that is available to organize the next festival. Combining different logics, temporalities and ambitions is the interesting friction that lies in front of us. In that sense the transition from Horst to ASIAT is not only a substantive but also an organizational challenge. We will have to drastically reinvent ourselves to deal with this new ambition and complexity."

52 "The city wants to develop the site in such a way that it becomes a more public space over time. A place that it always open. As a curator and manager of the site this will be challenging. From the moment we get the key we just have to start I think, open it up, let people passing by. We have to see how it grows, what goes wrong or slowly develops."

53 "For us it was an incredibly enjoyable experience. An experience where we learned a lot about how to be an architect for an institution. They functioned so well. We really totally got into that institution."

Tate Britain London

in conversation with
Adam Caruso

The renovation of a grand, late-Victorian building under heritage protection didn't suggest any daring interventions in the first instance. And yet it is precisely such interventions added to the existing built structure of the Tate Britain that have given the museum in London a new aesthetic and a new life. It is the small and precise details of form and materiality that make the transition from old to new seem almost natural.

From 2007 to 2013, Caruso St John Architects started to collaborate with Tate Britain for the masterplanning, upcoming renovations and possible future extensions of the renowned museum. Being appointed as the architects of the Tate implies a long-term commitment. The culture of trust and respect created the right conditions to question, challenge and collectively enable the institution to move with the times and to constantly reinvent itself and the definition of a museum.

What at first sight looks like a fine example of single authorship, ultimately reveals itself to be the collective effort of many involved, who together and in detail shaped new narratives for this building of cultural legacy.

Alongside delicate interventions, there were equally large and bold changes. How can such ideas be implemented within the rather rigid structure of an established institution? What role does the architect play in such a constellation? How can architecture help in representing a long-term, slow and ongoing reinvention of an institution?

Knowledge of the many

"At the Tate, they were never defensive. They were very open about what they needed, about what they were good at and about what they were bad at. They were really fantastic partners. At that time, more than 850 people were working there. So, you had this incredible constellation of people. Once a month, we would meet at director level and discuss the requirements for early years education, adult education, catering, retail, member space, shops, art spaces, fundraising and many more. In addition, as soon as the project became more detailed, there were end user meetings every week. They also had quite a sophisticated project management system. To give an example: it is the only project that I have ever worked on, where there was a useful risk register. It meant that on a project where we actually had a few disasters on-site and before, we were able to be on budget and more or less on time, because all of those things were built into the structure of how the project was managed before and during the construction."

TATE BRITAIN ARCHITECT
OJEU Restricted Procedure Notice 2006/S 107-114734
Interview/Presentation

Introduction
As part of the selection process you will be required to prepare a presentation and attend an interview. This will be held on Wednesday 22 November. We will contact you shortly to arrange the date and time for this.

Interview Panel
The Interview Panel has not yet been finalised but will include:

Sir Nicholas Serota	Director, Tate
Stephen Deuchar	Director, Tate Britain
Brian Gray	Director of Operations
Sir Jeremy Dixon	Partner, Jeremy Dixon & Edward Jones

Once we know the full membership of the panel, we will let you know.

Format
The interview will last for 50 minutes and will comprise a presentation by your team, followed by questions from the evaluation panel.

Presentation
You are being asked to make a 20 minute presentation that addresses the following brief. The panel are particularly interested to see how you approached the brief and how you arrived at the solutions you are presenting. You are not required to provide models or fully-worked drawings. The panel will want to see concept drawings and well considered solutions.
The presentation can be in any format and style of your choosing. If you wish to use Powerpoint it will be your responsibility to provide the equipment needed to facilitate the presentation. Four hard copies of the presentation should be available to the tender panel on the day of the presentation.
You should bring a team of no more than four people, including the director/principal who would be responsible for overseeing the contract and the architect who would act as day-to-day contact other team members.

Interview
The presentation will lead to a dialogue about the ideas in your presentation and a wider discussion about your approach to the appointment, including:

- Resourcing for the contract
- Client and stakeholder engagement
- Incorporating strategic objectives and the brief
- Ensuring design quality
- Co-ordination and design management

Preparation
You will be given an opportunity early in November to walk round the areas detailed in the brief accompanied by members of Tate staff. They will be able to answer any questions you might have. We will contact you shortly to arrange a suitable time for this.

Exercise for Presentation
Bringing Second Floor into Use
You are asked to consider the use of the Rotunda (the space above the main Millbank entrance).
You are being asked to prepare a presentation which:

- Describes your understanding of the issues involved in using this space
- Proposes a use for the space
- Considers questions of circulation of both people and materials
- Explains how the proposed use would fit in with the longer term masterplan for the Millbank site

The brief enclosed in the tender pack proposes that the new café will be sited in this space. You are not obliged to accept this proposal and are free to explore a different use of the space if you wish. However, your presentation will have to show that your alternative has taken into account both he Millbank development masterplan and the brief for Tate Britain.

54   "They told us: we are taking you on a year before we need to. And we are going to spend this money just to speculate about things together without any pressure. That is such a brilliant idea."

55   "With the conservation staff we were involved in really productive discussions on how to tackle things. We trusted each other. On some things they just said, that's a no-go, we can't do that. It doesn't matter what we think, it's just not possible, legally we can never approve it. On other things they followed us, like the fact that we replaced the whole floor in the rotunda in order to make it seem more part of the building."

"I guess it's really interesting to work with people in that way, when they respect you for what you're doing. You build up an incredible mutual respect, and I think in the end it's the only way you can make a really good project. The contact with the end user gives you this incredibly detailed knowledge of what's going on. I think architects can fill in a certain number of holes, but you can't replace a functioning client body, in the case of the Tate, an institution. Institutions that work are really things to be cherished, increasingly so, because obviously they've been under enormous pressure in the last few years. The Tate is so much more efficient than any developer we have worked with, beyond comparison."

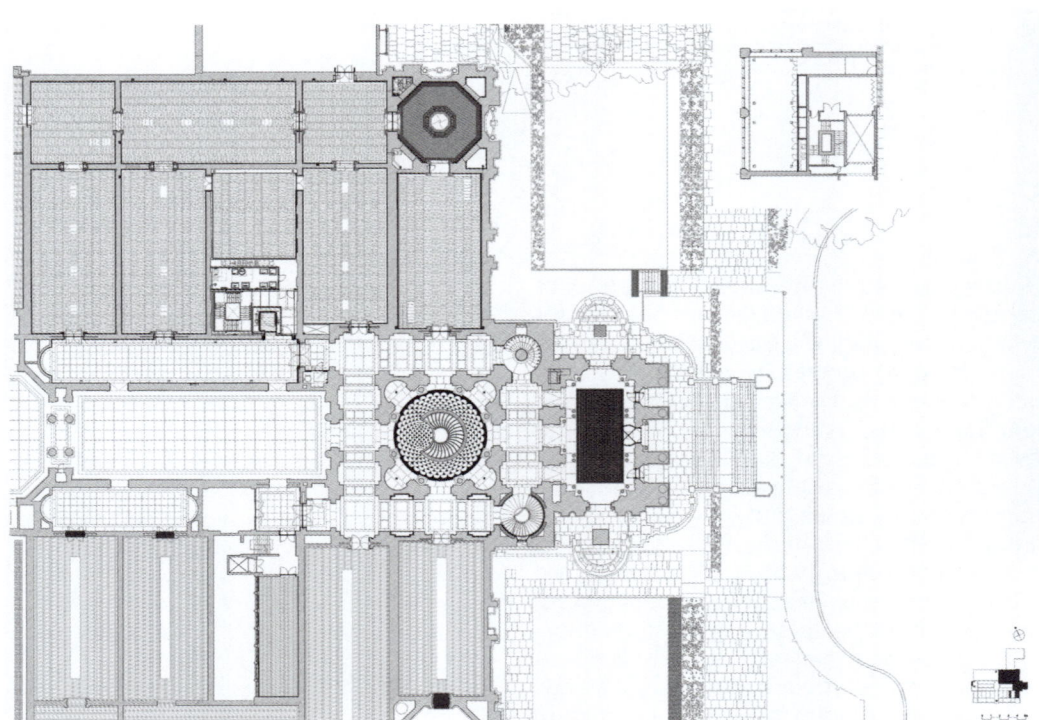

Safe ground for learning

"They did competitive interviews where you only had three weeks to prepare, so it really is not a competition, but more to see whether you get along with the institution. And they were very clear that they would be appointing the architect a year before they really needed him or her. And that was intentional. So, we had a year to work in a very speculative way. For example, we could first look at how big you would actually want Tate Britain to ever be. Together with the client, we did a number of thought experiments. How much of the collection would you ever want to show? How many entrances could you imagine the building to have on the Millbank site? We also looked at which part of the site could be developed as a commercial development to provide funding for an eventual third phase of our masterplan, which would be a new building. During this period, we produced a lot and discussed drafts and reports in a rigorous way every three weeks."

"Tate Britain has a tradition of working with an architect for twenty years. The previous architect was John Miller. I met him a few times. We had a special meeting at the beginning, where they kind of, metaphorically, handed over the keys of the building to us. This long-term commitment made it possible to discuss and plan things together over months and years. The design was no longer just ours, but a result that everyone involved in the process had internalized, and could argue for. This also applied to the rotunda. It was really an effective way of dealing with all sorts of things that our project was about. But as soon as we did that stair, it obviously had to be the most beautiful stair in the world. Luckily, we did not have to design it in a rush. We had five and a half years to design that stair and we took all five and a half years. We did prototypes and we had a traffic planner check if the stair would not block the ways into, and around the Tate."

Risky experiments

"There were big questions, like the stair in the rotunda, which was very significant—but which was also an incorrect thing to do in terms of classicism. There is no precedent for making such a big hole and stair in the middle of a classical rotunda."

"The Tate re-invents itself institutionally. I think in a museum, this is common and necessary. It is impressive how the Tate balances public and private funding, and how in the themes for exhibitions there is a constant balancing between loss-making and making money. It's about the mixture. Somebody comes to the popular show and then maybe goes to see the young artist or mid-career artist which they wouldn't have seen otherwise."

56 "The Tate was very clear about what it wanted to get. Tate members have their own council. I would meet with them, we would talk about the design, but we would also talk about how the members wanted their special spaces to work. It's cheap to be a member. I'm a Tate member. There're over a hundred thousand members, so it's meant to be an emancipatory thing. It's like a kind of microcosm of society."

57 "You don't have discussions about everything, it is too complex. You've done a masterplan, you've done an outline design; everybody understands that you're not going to radically change these things, which would be quite disruptive."

58 "Good clients never want you to design in the way it is now, they are always thinking about the future. And when you challenge them with something that they never imagined, they are usually slightly shocked, but then also really excited."

59 "The client and certain potential funders said, well, it should be a glass stair, because then it disappears, and you do not see it. I had to say, no, I do not think it should be a glass stair, we are in this rather lumpy late-Victorian building, everything is heavy, and we need to do something which somehow lifts this architecture."

60 "Sometimes the work with artists is very collaborative and sometimes we just facilitate their project. Like making a good gallery, judgement is needed to support the artist's specific project."

Senior improvisor

"This open-minded approach to work allows us to get involved with the ideas and visions of others and to take the time needed, regardless of economic gain or loss. It allows us to gain insights into the work of clients and their very different agendas. This leads to productive collaborations, which we also have in other projects, like the one for Deutsche Werkstätten Hellerau, where our architecture is being used as a test for different processes of design and manufacturing. The experiences of these different projects make you become more open, because if you only were doing projects for developers that had a very clear and deterministic timeline, I guess you would not really know how to engage with these other processes. Trusting your intelligence in a way to be able to navigate these situations, is always interesting."

Culture of cooperation

"The real parallel with the Tate is that we also try to make sure everyone is empowered. At the end of the project, three artists were directly commissioned to work in the entrance foyer and the new café space. The sculptor, Nicole Wermers designed a spoon, which did not require too much of involvement from our side. Richard Wright's window in the main entrance foyer, however, demanded intensive collaboration to achieve a very subtle effect within the given time and financial conditions. Some architects would have said, you are ruining my architecture, but with the Tate and us, we weren't really thinking that way."

61   "In Greece it's all about the ancient and Byzantine stuff. We tend to forget the recent history. But this is the history that has formed the contemporary identity. We have to cherish it, make its materiality part of our everyday life."

Communitism Athens

in conversation with
Natassa Dourida

Communitism is a community space located in the central Athens district of Metaxourgio. It fascinates through the combination of the charm of a historical neo-classical building, colorful art, a diverse community, a relaxed atmosphere and the feeling of belonging. Yet, Communitism is much more than just a space. It is a multi-layered project, with the aim of reactivating precious, dilapidated buildings. It conveys the recognition of art as a valuable profession and a legitimate means of expression, which as a common language succeeds in conveying ideas and opening up possibilities for joint action. Within the framework of funding and educational programs of European cultural institutes, the project was initially conceived as an experiment. Consisting of three consecutive events, the idea was to initiate a process that would, through open, slow and collective learning processes, in the long-term lead to the construction of a self-sustaining community space.

How can a safe space from many individuals with different motivations pursue such a clear vision for creating added value in Athens? How were individual ideologies reconciled with the claim of radical openness? How could collective learning processes be made consistent with roles and responsibilities?

Out of necessity

"I could not find the motivation to work as a civil engineer, having more concrete buildings making Athens even vaster and even more chaotic. So, I started from my personal need to do something of positive value for the society. Athens is grey, crumbling and it gives us this feeling that we do not deserve something good. So, I thought that I want to participate, to offer my knowledge in a positive way. And this is why I decided to do my master's in restoration of monuments, always thinking that it is the recent history that we need to bring out, to keep alive."

62   "You have to design it so that people can see how they can use it, but by being there, we could also see how we can use it. It was a very self-generated situation. One day we felt like bringing down the wall that connects the two apartments. In reality these actions did not feel like design."

"In 2009, the neighborhood of Metaxourgio, characterized by neoclassical building fabric, was becoming what it is today: a next centre of the city. It started having many 'do-it-yourself' cafés and taverns that were quite cheap. One could get the feeling that each one of us could start one of them. These cafés were not very formal, not very expensive and not very professional places. Well-educated people, interested in the arts, interested in new means of communication, all willing to put their efforts in creating alternative ways of living, came together. There were many of them by then, they were a community already."

Knowledge of the many

"I got inspired by travelling, conversations with international Airbnb guests, existing cultural centers in Germany and the secluded community-organized Greek island Ikaria. I was telling my friend that I needed to find a way to do something and at some point she sent me an open call of a cultural management fellowship, from the Robert-Bosch-Stiftung along with the Greek Goethe Institute. They were looking for people with a degree, any degree, and a creative idea. I thought: 'Okay, since they want a creative idea, a cultural idea, it could be a socio-cultural center'. And this is exactly what Communitism is."

"A central idea is that communities can work together, create systems, and then these systems can affect other systems. Not as a revolution, because a revolution is a reaction. I don't want a reaction, I want a creation, a self-generated creation. The experiment was that through three events, we would start whirling around. By whirling around, you expect to create a field, you know, where other people will come in and participate and play their roles."

63   "Through Communitism I have found people that I consider my tribe."

"There should be a system of exchange so that the owners have something to gain by allowing me to work on their buildings."

Risky experiments

"The stakes were high. We wanted to develop our own cultural commons. The experiment claimed that after three events, with three different communities, we would have a building, the legal structure, the community and the business plan to have an operational collective space in Athens, and that for the very first time."

Safe ground for learning

"The success of the first two events exceeded the manageable workload. After the third we had a real crisis, because we overextended ourselves. Metaphorically speaking: I considered myself to be the mother, and Communitism to be my baby, and we had reached a point where the baby had grown up, but I had not understood it yet, that I was still mothering it. Suddenly there were legal obligations and real responsibilities, and the naivety was gone. From being an organic group of people, we moved towards a structure, organized by weekly team meetings, a board, a plenum and elections. At the same time, I became aware that only by taking me out as the initiator of the system and by allowing others to grow into new responsibilities, the very core idea of Communitism, to be a collective learning process, could be maintained."

65 "I believed that not everyone should be in for the big idea. One space was a filthy storage of old book cases. When we saw it, the first idea was to shut the room, but there were three women who were obsessed with turning it into a kitchen. They were buying tablecloths and bringing flowers up to a point that I told them to stop. We still had another 1,000 square meters to renovate."

66 "Each one of us has their personal motivations. it's something very pragmatic. It is ok to not be inspired by the bigger vision, because you can get lost in it, you can lose yourself in it."

67 "In exchange of having a gallery, an artist took care about moisture issues and the cockroaches. Another girl asked to do a cinema, others to create a free shop. So, this is how the first three spaces happened. All of it is participatory design, organic growth."

68 "It was the carnival of 2009 that brought Metaxourgio together. I remember telling a friend of mine that I need to do something here. I told him I had to find a way to save these buildings from decay."

Senior improvisor

"Despite not having institutional funding, we held on to the idea of organizing three events. The owner of the first building, a former carpentry business, was looking for solutions after having gone bankrupt. They were clearly politically right wing. This is when I understood that I should not be using any kind of familiar political vocabulary, because I wanted us to connect on the basis of finding solutions. We could not be preaching the death of capitalism or whatever. In the end he trusted the idea for the first event. When electricity was cut off four days before the event, he even allowed for it to be illegally reconnected."

"The step-by-step approach and financial constraints forced us to focus on one event at a time. It was always about the now. Looking back, this permitted an organic growth of the community, not only for the three events, but also for the communication with the owners. With the owners of the second building, who were willing to host the next events, a three-steps agreement says to first deal with the building's maintenance, then with restoration and finally with long-term solutions. As a result, I'm currently doing the studies, like a doctor, to see where it hurts. I really don't know where this will lead to."

Culture of cooperation

"Even though, especially initially, much was done through contacts, friends and mutual give and take, there were certain basic rules. One of these was the ensured provision of a fee, albeit small and symbolic, for artists. It was also part of recognizing the fact that artists must be able to live off their profession, and that we shouldn't be inflicting on ourselves what society already does, asking us to work for free."

69 "Our business plan is not only about how we deal with money, rather it is an economic model, where economy is the way you regulate your house. Writing that plan was actually the most collective process of writing we have ever had."

When we built the Design in Dialogue Lab at ETH Zurich in 2019, we tried to create the necessary safe space to deal with and learn about the challenges described in this publication. Combining theatrical elements (lights, curtains, props) with tools for co-production, including a mobile kitchen, the lab offers a variety of spatial configurations that allow us to share experiences, test new ideas, try out new practices and to reflect, share and relax.

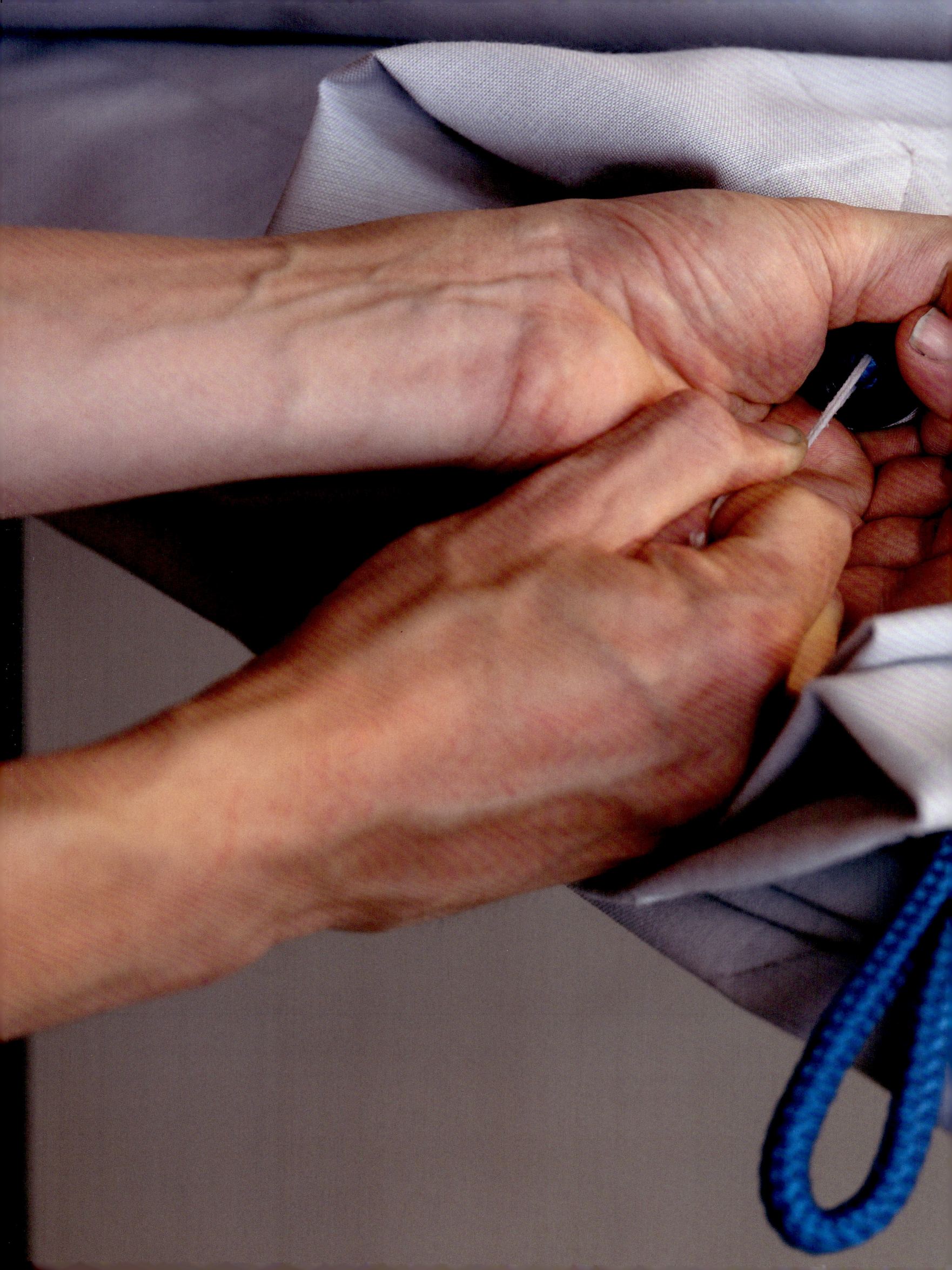